M000234404

Power Exchange Books' Resource Series

PROTOCOLS:
a Variety of Views

Published by The Nazca Plains Corporation
Las Vegas, Nevada
2008

ISBN: 978-1-934625-87-3

Published by

The Nazca Plains Corporation ®
4640 Paradise Rd, Suite 141
Las Vegas NV 89109-8000

Cover, Photos by Corwin
Art Director, Blake Stephens

Power Exchange Books' Resource Series

PROTOCOLS:
a Variety of Views

Series Editor, Dr. Bob (Bob Rubel)
Issue Coordinator, L.C. Morgynn

Foreword

From Dr. Bob (Bob Rubel), the Series Editor

As many of you know, the topic of protocols is near and dear to my heart. I live in a 24/7 protocol-heavy Master/slave relationship, and am quite comfortable with that, thank you.

However, not all Families use protocols. Those that do use protocols in their relationship range from using only a few protocols to having an extensive *Protocol Manual* written out for the slave's use. I hasten to point out that those who use common Leather protocols may use them slightly differently, based on the part of the country in which they live. One often hears about "East Coast versus West Coast" styles of protocols. Also, many Masters or Doms make up their own protocols as befits that particular relationship.

It is my intent, with this issue to print articles from Masters and slaves that represent divergent views. More importantly, many of these articles discuss the philosophical basis for the way protocols have developed within their Family.

The reason that protocols vary so much between Families is that *protocols* serve a few important aspects of a power exchange or authority exchange relationship:

- Protocols give the Master/Dom an opportunity to shape the daily structure of life with a slave/submissive. Protocols can be used to enforce deference and respect; they can be used to make the relationship look very different from a vanilla relationship; they can be used to clarify communication between partners.

- Written protocols really represent the specifics of the ways that Master/Dom wants slave/submissive to behave. It's rather a "manual for living with Master." This can be very helpful for the slave or submissive, as it clearly sets forth what Master expects from slave. Thus, slave has specific ways he/she knows to behave to please Master. And, *pleasing Master* is what the relationship is all about, yes?

Interesting stuff, at least for me.

So, I hope you enjoy this book, and also the entire Resource Series that I put out. All books in this series can be obtained from:

www.PowerExchangeBooks.com

In Leather Heart and Spirit,

Dr. Bob

Future Books in this Series

We are actively seeking writers and issue coordinators for topics that can be found at: www.powerexchangebooks.com/Kim/upcoming.html. ; If you are interested in participating with any of these titles, please write to Bob Rubel at: PowerExchangeEditor@Yahoo.com for more details.

Contents

Preface

by L.C. Morgynn

I used to have a very low opinion of protocols. From what I saw of them, protocols were fantasy-based, almost invariably sexual in nature, and only used in online roleplay and by those whose knowledge of the BDSM lifestyle was limited to fantasy scenarios. Then, at the urging of an acquaintance, I read Robert Rubel's Protocols: Handbook for the female slave (Nazca Plains, 2006). What an eye-opener! I instantly became the biggest proponent of protocols that can be found, and I have continued to pursue a strong interest in the subject. I see protocols, now, as crucial; one of the foundations of a successful Master/slave relationship.

This book contains a collection of essays representing the writings of a few Masters and slaves presenting widely divergent views of protocols and how/why they are used as they are from the authors' perspectives.

The book opens with Sergeant Major's contribution on how he defines a protocol, and the uses of protocols in the mundane world, and how they translate and how they translate to our Lifestyle.

This is followed by Raven Ryker's account of what it was like for him to be in on the process of development and implementation of his Master's household protocols, and his adjustment from understanding protocols as a concept alone, to the reality of living with protocols.

Master Tallen creates a strong argument for the effective

use of Protocols, and he goes into some details as to the how and why protocols work; what it is about protocols that make them a cornerstone of the Master/slave relationship, and how protocols are motivational for both Master and slave.

Sir Stephen defines protocols as they are used in his household. He covers the basic functions that he considers protocols should serve, and emphasizes simplicity and practical usefulness.

Cecelia S. likens protocols to etiquette, making some extremely powerful arguments for treating others, both Dominants and submissives alike, with respect within the community at large. She stresses what, really, would be – in most non-Lifestyle venues – considered mere common courtesy! For instance, a Dominant should not treat a submissive as his own when she is not, merely because she is submissive. Nor should a submissive feel bound to serve any Master who is not hers, for the sole reason that he is Dominant.

Slave elizabeth gives us a close look at the rather unique protocols and M/s structure of her Master, Jack McGee, who puts his own stamp of determination on what a Master/slave household looks like. Her account may raise a few eyebrows, and may also engender intense envy from some slaves reading this piece.

Eric Pride touches briefly on the history of usage of protocols. He then goes on to define and comment on the various purposes that protocols may serve, such as communication, speech patterns, etc.

The article by Obsidian, he discusses a simple construct for building your own protocols. He also discusses rituals and how they are different from protocols, and how to enhance protocols by adding ritual to create a smoothly integrated structure for interaction between Master and slave, that serves them on a daily basis.

Tala Thera offers us a very personal look at protocols; what they mean to her, and how the use of protocols creates a special bond between herself and her Master. She also gives us a brief glimpse of what it is like when the Master himself may, for some reason, lose sight of an established protocol, thus underscoring the point, often overlooked, that protocols are as much for the Master as the slave!

In a second article, Sergeant Major provides us with a window into his own household protocols, referring to them by the military term "SOP" or "standard operating procedures." There are specific examples of protocols he has established for use with his slaves, in particular the process that a slave goes through to petition for slavery, through the collaring ceremony.

Cassy Horrocks gives us some simple rules of BDSM etiquette. In my opinion, this should be mandatory reading for all of us living this lifestyle. While you would think that just basic good "manners" would be all that would be required; sadly, many people seem not to correlate the manners that one hoped they learned at their mother's knee, with how to behave properly in a dungeon or play party or any other kind of BDSM/lifestyle event. Cassy brings this to us with a clarity that is well worth reading, and passing on.

The book ends with an amusing, light-hearted spoof of BDSM spirituality, presented by Graydancer in "The 10 Commandments of Kink."

In summary, protocols can be used to create a structure that keeps the M/s relationship alive, not just day-to-day but moment-to-moment, and over both time and distance. Protocols keep the Master/slave hierarchy in place, and also keep the Master and slave both continually aware of their respective status, so that they don't wake up one morning and find themselves in a vanilla, albeit slightly kinky, relationship instead of Lifestyle.

It was my own continuing pursuit on the subject that led me to contact Dr. Bob in regards to using Protocols: Handbook for the female slave in a local book discussion group. That, in turn, led eventually to his asking me to be the Issue Coordinator for this book. I was both pleased and amazed, and highly honored to be able to contribute in some way to the publication of this work.

About the Author:

L.C. Morgynn is known as "CatWhoWalksAlone" in her local BDSM community and online, and "slaveheart cat" in the larger MAsT community. Having spent 12 years as "Lady Morgynn," a Fem Domme, in early 1997 she made the startling discovery that she had a slave heart, and since then has learned to accept, and then embrace, her slave nature. Although unowned, she pursues a highly visible activism in her local community of Greensboro, N. Carolina, as well as being involved in MAsT (Masters And slaves Together). She attended the fifth female slave training class at Master Taino's Training Academy in 2008, and her first-ever lifestyle conference, the Master/slave Conference in Washington, D.C., that same year. She has a strong belief in the need for community, networking and outreach. Her website is www.farhorizons.net/cat and she can be reached at cat@farhorizons.net.

Question: An established code of conduct. Answer: What is a protocol?

By Sergeant Major

While not really a Jeopardy question, not knowing or understanding protocols can get us into social jeopardy. The simplest meaning is that a protocol is a preset way of doing things.

We are faced with protocols every day, from the ones involved in common courtesy to our IP (internet protocol) address. There are medical protocols, computer protocols, diplomatic protocols and those that go by the name of standard operating procedure. In design all have as their foundation an attempt to create a standard way of doing things to prevent errors and misunderstandings. In addition they can be designed to demonstrate hierarchy, loyalty and service.

To apply this to a power exchange relationship, several different avenues or approaches are available. We can use them as a way of structuring the relationship, as a way of creating ritual in the relationship, and as a way of demonstrating our relationship to others. Each of these has multiple ways of being demonstrated and every master will have a different set of rules and procedures they want to have followed. These can vary from the Miss Manners code of etiquette through the military model to the mystical world of Gor. There is no right set of protocols for all relationships, since the personas of the ones in the relationship will determine what will work for them. The value of a protocol is that it provides a set of guidelines for how certain things are to be done. Those who know and follow a particular protocol have something in common, a predictable set of guidelines which have a standard outcome.

By creating and using protocols we establish how we want things done in a certain sequence or certain situations. How do we wish those who are in our household to interact with other both within and without the household? How are they to interact with us in the various different situations with which we are confronted in everyday life, since we can not always be in role? How do we want them to demonstrate to others the role they have chosen to follow when in lifestyle-specific situations? Do we want to have different protocols for different things which we do, for example in a social gathering as opposed to a dungeon, or when preparing for a scene? These are individual or household protocols; in addition we can have protocols which will govern how we act as members of a club or organization.

What are some guidelines for establishing protocols? We each bring our personal preferences, biases and expectations to the protocols we create. In all cases there has to be a reason for a procedure to be a part of an overall protocol or it will not be observed. To begin, decide the various categories for which you want to establish protocols. Categories can include daily routines, conduct in public, conduct at social events and conduct outside of the household. Not every master will choose to address any or all of these examples; simply choose or create those which you find apply to your situation. When categories have been decided, it is easier to establish appropriate protocols for each one.

In the category of daily routines you can have a set procedure for beginning each day with a greeting or affirmation ritual. Positions to be assumed for certain activities or actions can be created and employed. How the members of the household address you when in private versus in public is specified. In a multi-partner household the hierarchy of those pledged is assigned. How the pledged members of the household dress when at home is a protocol. A daily schedule of activities of a continuing nature is a protocol, as are certain required tasks.

Conduct in public can have two separate sets of protocols, one for when accompanying the master and another set for when unaccompanied. Rather than trying to give examples here I think it better to pose questions. Where do you want them to stand in relationship to you? What position are they to assume when standing in your presence? Do you want their hands in sight or hidden? Are they to sit on furniture when you are sitting? What services are they to provide, and when? When not accompanying you how are they to conduct themselves? What if any symbolic representation of their pledge is to be displayed in public? What are their instructions with regard to interacting with others? What terms of address will they use?

Conduct at social events can be based on standard forms of etiquette with lifestyle-specific ones added for those times when they are appropriate. There is a wide variation in the types of social events associated with the lifestyle, from formal dinners to munches to club dining out events. For most, the protocols established for conduct in public will apply, while also allowing those which cannot be comfortably used in more vanilla settings. Protocols involving kneeling, sitting on the floor at your feet and the various submissive actions and postures are more appropriate at lifestyle events. Here is where the protocols can demonstrate the nature of the relationship to others. They will also indicate the style of the relationship as to its underlying philosophy; for example, manners-based, military-based or something else. More formal events will have their own set of protocols developed and required by the group conducting the formal events.

Protocols for conduct outside of the household are designed to remind the members of their relationship but not draw undo attention when they are at work or in a situation totally divorced from the lifestyle. These can include covert symbols of their pledge, required preset contacts, or even special terms of address having meaning only to the persons using them. These can often be the most difficult to establish and execute.

Protocols are ways of enhancing and defining lifestyle relationships by creating a unique set of procedures and practices for each household. They cover everyday conduct and formal situations and the ways the relationship can exist and be practiced in the world of work and non-lifestyle situations. Their value lies not only in the practical aspect of being standardized and predictable, but also in their mental, emotional and philosophical aspects. The time spent developing and following them will be the key to the value they have for any relationship. The primary element in good protocols is simplicity in execution and applicability to the situations in which the members of the household find themselves. Overly complex protocols may play well in a written form but will not always work well in practice. Creating or requiring a protocol to be learned and then not following it simply creates a situation which can demean the others by causing them to be doubted as to their validity.

Well thought out and constructed protocols will demonstrate the competence and command of the master. Well executed protocols will demonstrate the intelligence, capability and value of the submissive.

Question: Relationship parameters setting out what is right or wrong or possible and impossible which strengthen and define a relationship.

Answer: What are protocols?

About the Author:

A committed follower of the leather tradition, Sergeant Major has taken on paying forward to those who want to learn in order to repay those who took the time to teach him. Dedicated to preserving the traditions of brotherhood, honesty, trust and loyalty which are the hallmarks of the leather tradition into the 21st Century by sharing them with those who want to go beyond the gateway of the lifestyle. Serving in his community as a teacher, mentor and worker and leading by example as a master. Proud to be honoured by having slave riches pledged to him.

Memberships:
MAsT: Twin Cities
Minnesota Leather Pride Committee
STL3, St Louis
Associate member, Atons of Minneapolis
Associate member, Chicago Leather Club

Protocols: A Slave's Perspective

By Raven Rykers

As a slave, I always thought that I wanted and needed protocols. A step-by-step description of how to do what I was supposed to do to be a good slave or to know exactly what was expected of me in service. I thought, "Just get the rules and follow them." It sounded so easy. I never really thought about how this was supposed to happen or what went into the process. Basically I had figured that this was a fool-proof way to avoid mistakes or failure. All I had to do was follow the protocols. Of course, that was how it worked in the stories I read and even those I made up in my head. Well, I forgot that nothing comes without a price. I had not counted on the various ways I would be impacted by protocols. I was quite surprised by my reactions and how they evolved over time. Just as protocols themselves are fluid and evolve. I was just beginning to understand the path I was on.

I had the privilege of being a part of the creation process for a set of household protocols. I have a much deeper respect for the time, effort and emotion that go into designing a workable set of protocols. The first step, which turned out to be the longest, involved sitting down and writing out what the goals of the protocols were going to be. In the process of writing down my owner's thoughts — and trying to design wording that communicated the idea — I found my own questions adding to the mix. Over and over, I would ask what this rule meant. I found I was interested in the **why** behind them;

not because I was questioning the rule, but because I found that once I understood why Sir or Ma'am wanted something done this particular way, I would be emotionally invested in giving them what they wanted. It was an aligning of heart and mind in obedience. It helped me to understand the goals in my own service. I guess it could be called the subtle difference between compliance and obedience. This was the thing that gave me the most profound sense of just how much meaning goes into having a set of protocols and the feelings that come from living within them.

I was completely surprised by my own reaction to the process. Getting to discuss the thoughts and reasons and the desired effect made me feel so much more invested in the success I desired for both my owner and myself. I found I was looking to the protocols as much more than a simple blue print of my actions. They were ritualistic in nature and repeated as each situation arises. These were frequently actions or phrases that reaffirm each person's role in the relationship. They were designed to create a mood, teach a specific behavior, achieve a specific goal or even simply because it pleases the owner to have it that way. Seeing them in this way gave me a deeper sense of pride in myself as a slave.

Once the goals were sorted out, it moved into how does Sir or Ma'am word the protocols. There was a precision to this effort that spoke of the pride and beliefs that went into them. I knew my owner wanted them to be understandable and clear. I wanted that as well, and yes, there was a self interest type of desire involved. Who wouldn't want a framework that gives them clearly defined boundaries in which to serve? It was equally important that the wording reflect a sense of grace and respect for both the servant and the served. After a few trial approaches, my owner elected to keep the wording of the protocol in the positive such as "do walk" as opposed to the negative "don't run" style. I discovered in having positively worded set of protocols for my actions made them easier to remember and it also made me more eager to follow. It also felt like forward movement in my emotional world because I was able to feel the exchange of power between myself and my owner. I was embodying my owner's desires. Of course, I did not always hold this understanding about protocols. It was a journey.

I still didn't fully grasp everything that protocols offered me, but I was gaining ground. I was more and more eager to learn them, to get them right. I wanted to do the right thing and to please my owner in my service. Most every slave I have ever spoken to about service has similar feelings. I understood it was what was required of me and it would please my owner. I just had to realize what I got beyond the feelings of "I did a good job." They fed me in a different way as well. I didn't have the words to describe it yet. My next step in understanding took me in a new direction.

Once the household had a functional set of protocols I began to commit them to memory. They covered the mundane day to day operation of a home and expanded outward to encompass our actions within our community. Of course some were more exciting than others. They gave me the information I needed to function in my owner's home and be a positive part of the household. How does Sir or Ma'am want tasks done? When should these things happen? What do I do if I have questions or if I am unsure? How do I behave in any given situation? What rituals were daily versus less often?

So began the next step of the living with the protocols. This turned out to be both a practical application and an emotionally charged endeavor for me. There were several revisions for some in order to achieve the goals and still be sustainable. Others were dropped when they either no longer served my owners purpose or simply didn't work as once predicted. Many had no reason behind them except that they were what pleased my owner. It was practice, practice, practice.

I, of course, was in a high energy state. It was exciting and new. I was filled with an energy that made each action special. I was doing all the things I had merely longed for. I was finally in what I had always felt was my natural place. It turned out to be what I later heard called the honeymoon phase. I had read many books and I had my own ideas of what serving was going to be like and now I was actually doing it. This was exciting. This was very erotic at times. Wait, this was work. I had not expected to have it feel this way at all. It never worked like that in my imagination. I had not counted on fantasy and reality coming together like that. I began to have doubts about my chosen role. I felt a bit let down and confused. Why were the protocols not continuing to give me the elated feelings?

I had come to recognize that my imagined ideas about what protocols were and the reality of them were two different things. Sometimes protocols were not going to be all about graceful kneeling or walking quietly behind my owner. It wasn't all storybook fantasy. Sometimes they were about how to do chores the way my owner wanted them done. I was, to say the least, confused by the change in feelings about protocols. I missed the earlier excitement. How did this happen? Where did it go? I was feeling the weight of the protocols like fetters. I followed them but it wasn't as fulfilling as I had imagined.

This is the place where I realized that I was now following the protocols out of what I call compliance. It was following the letter of the law, but not the intent of the law. I did exactly what was expected and I generally did it well, however an important piece was missing. When I realized the shine had worn off I looked outside to see how it had happened and how to get it back. It took a while for me to gain the perspective I needed to get past this place. I began to grasp that even the mundane tasks were important and would be fulfilling when I got the why I was doing it sorted out in both my head and my heart. I discovered it was within me that the change had occurred and it was within me I would find the answer. I had to let go of my preconceived ideas. I was feeling the protocols as a burden to be borne instead of seeing them as a celebration of our relationship. My own pride and stubborn will were battling for balance, as if only one could survive, instead of me seeking fulfillment in my role through obedience. Many, many long talks with my owner and other slaves happened during this growth phase. Thankfully my owner was a patient sort.

I then began to see that protocols were more than a mere blueprint for my actions. It wasn't just a set of rules to follow. These were, each in their way, a ritual. Each prescribed behavior served more than getting the laundry done and the socks put away in the magic sock drawer. They gave me reassurance of what my place was in the relationship. They told me each time I was an owned slave. They also gave my owner the same types of things, including clean socks.

Over time it became a way of living that felt natural. I was allowing the part of me to flourish that was my will surrendering to my owners will. I discovered that surrender did not mean death for my will. It became more and more clear that doing it right was good, but it was doing in the right frame of mind and heart that mattered.

The protocols were instructive to be sure, but they also were comforting and were a way for me to have positive input and feedback on how I was doing in service. I had a clear way of understanding exactly what was expected of me and the formulas to achieve these goals. I also knew if I had fallen short of these goals. In a way it helped me keep my internal rheostat set at the proper position.

The protocols also gave me a clear sense of consequences for my actions. They gave me both the plans for behavior and the explained what the outcome for falling short would be. This, while sounding a tad more ominous than it may have been, did a couple of things for me as a slave. I was comforted by knowing that there was a set of consequences for my actions. A part of service for me is also submitting to another's will and decisions. A large part of that submission is accepting my behavior will be determined by another and that I will answer to them for both positive and negative situations.

Now I should mention that in my past I have been in service to others who have already set down their protocols before I ever arrived at their household. Likewise I have been on loan to households with differing protocols in place. I wanted to follow these rules in the same manner. I wanted to get it right, and I found walking into a known set of protocols at least gave me a complete sense of knowing what you were getting into. I do not think I lost anything in coming to these situations after the ideas and goals were set down. It was different than the things I experienced by being a part of the creation of them. Perhaps it was the difference in compliance with the rules in the beginning and growing into my obedience as my understanding grew, and the feeling of it being a much faster movement towards obedience getting to see protocols from inception.

I believe that in the first stages of forming your will to match another's there is a time of compliance to the letter of the law followed by obedience to the intent of the law. I have come to understand I do have a period of getting my mind to know and follow a protocol that will lead my heart to realign to that same goal. I also understand I do this more quickly if I understand the why behind it as much as the what or how.   I think being more involved in the process has given me a deeper understanding of each of these parts of my reactions to protocols.

Protocols were much more than a simple way to do what my owner wanted. They were a framework to live within, a set of boundaries. They also were a fertile ground to grow in. My growth may have been guided and pruned just so, but I was indeed thriving and growing. I was now seeing the inherent freedom of the fetters I had once thought the protocols were.

I have come full circle on how I am affected by protocols. I am back to the feeling of wonder and excitement. I recognize protocols as being the place where my growth in a relationship begins. They are an important brick in the foundation. They do not need to be elaborate or extensive. They simply need to recognized for all the things they bring to a relationship.

About the Author:

I am a 40-something service-oriented slave who identifies also as a butch leather dyke, living in Albuquerque. While I am currently not in an M/s relationship, I have been in several long term 24/7 service relationships. I have talked on M/s and BDSM topics at many events including South Plains Leather Fest, Black Rose, Rio Grande Leather and the M/s Conference. I held the 2005 NE slave title.

I can be reached at rrykers@aol.com

Protocols in BDSM and Leather: The Invisible Leash

By Master Tallen

I am a firm believer in communication, whether it is in a relationship, in general, or in our community. But in order to communicate effectively, the parties involved should be speaking the same language and they should have the same definitions of words. My observation is that this is not happening in our community. For example, the words I just used; "our community." What do you think I mean? The BDSM community? The Leather Community? Well, for My purposes today, I am speaking of the Master/slave community, and more precisely, the Master/slave lifestyle community. Now that I have made that clear, I will explain what I mean when I use the word, "protocol." For me, protocols are rules that a Master establishes for slaves in His/Her service to follow regarding posture and behavior. This includes general behavior and speech, but would not include such things as how to wash the dishes or fold the clothes. Those are entirely different regulations, policies, or procedures. Too many times, Masters tend to clutter up their protocols with irrelevant rules and procedures. Those should be kept in another category so you do not make the mistake of setting the slave up for failure. For the most part, slaves in our community share two common fears: failure and rejection. Masters should make great effort to ensure that slaves are successful in their service, and in their primary goal of pleasing the Master. One of the best ways I have found to help in this endeavor is by establishing and maintaining protocols. The

15

strongest desire for a slave is to please the Master. So, why not give them basic information of how the Master expects the slave to behave. In polls I have taken, 100% of slaves have stated that they need the master to have written protocols. At the same time, Masters polled, report that only 25% of them have written protocols. This deficit should be corrected. In My opinion, Masters should drop their egos, and give the slaves the basic tools with which to operate.

To me, protocols are the foundation of the Master/slave dynamic. In addition to giving the slave guidelines and a foundation in which the slave can refer to in order to ensure the performance the Master desires, there are many other reasons to have protocols. Most Masters agree that by having a slave follow their protocols they feel respect from the slave. A slave who follows his/her Master's protocols avoids failure because the decisions of how to behave in situations have already been made by the Master.

By creating these basic guidelines the Master expresses how He/She desires a slave to behave, thus achieving clarity of His/Her wishes. It ensures that the Master will get the desired results in just about any situation. By having a list of guidelines to follow, the slave feels the guidance and control of the Master without the Master having to be present or verbally dictate the slave's every move. This is the primary reason I like to refer to protocols and as the invisible leash.

A Master affirms His/Her mastery by taking possession of a slave and/or placing the collar on his property. A slave affirms his/her slavery by accepting the Master's collar or ownership. Reaffirmation is that element of the dynamic in which each is reminded of his or her place. Protocols are another tool that is used to reaffirm the slave's place as property of the Master. In addition, they remind the Master of His/Her place as owner. For example, one protocol that I have is that slaves in My service do not use foul language. Every time an instance arises in which a slave could use a curse word and they do not, they immediately think of me. This reminds them of their place and further instills my control upon them and I do not have to be present. Another simple example would be that during toilet usage slaves sit on the toilet rim and do not use the seat. I as a Master will stand to pee, the slave will not. Therefore, every time the slave performs this basic life function they are reminded of their place in life. Knowing this, the Master is reminded of His/Her place. Anytime you can take advantage of everyday functions and use them to benefit their relationship you should do so. That is not to say that all of us need to have the same protocols. We do not. What works for me and My dynamic may not work for you, and that is OK. All we need to do is to take what works for us and use those tools to the best of our ability.

By maintaining protocols, the Master and slave share a connection. If you have ever had a best friend or family member that you share an inside joke with, then you can relate to the type of connection that protocols can give to the Master and slave. It is that moment when something happens in a crowded room that incites a certain feeling in you that only the other person senses too. When I walk down the street and My slave is in protocol following to My right and a half a step behind, it excites me that: one, I am in control of this person, and two, no one else knows it.

This may sound strange, but along with the connection, protocols create separation. Meaning, the slave is separated from the Master and other superiors, thus further reaffirming the slave's position in life. For example, the standard protocol that slaves do not use furniture is a way of showing that Masters and slaves are not equal, thus separating them.

Master or slave can create protocols. It is up to the Master to decide which ones He/She wants. In establishing your own protocols there are many things to consider. By doing research and attending workshops at the various conferences that have sprung up around the country, you can learn different variations in protocols. Assess your own needs and desires and apply what you've learned, and what you want, to your protocols. For me, My protocols say who I am and what I want. They are pretty much nonnegotiable. However, it is sometimes necessary to compromise to accommodate possible limits or limitations of slaves I encounter. In addition, there have been instances in My journey as a master that slaves in My service have introduced protocols for My approval. Some of those were accepted by me, and some were not. It can be very helpful to a master for a slave to introduce protocols because a slave, as a person, has more insight to their own personality than the Master ever will. The slaves, having inside information as to what guidelines or actions many more effectively feed them, would be providing an invaluable service by bringing this to the Master's attention. Establishing a protocol and later changing it to suit you, does not make you weak or unintelligent in the eyes of the slave. Moreover, it would confirm in the slave's mind that you know what you want and how to get it. You should start with basics such as speech, and develop your list from there. Be sure to keep your protocols basic guidelines for behavior, and do not include chores and duties. They are separate issues. Ask yourself the question, "If I had a slave here right now, what would I have him/her doing, and how would I have them doing it?"

As with other rules and/orders you dictate to your slave, enforcing your protocols is imperative. A slave will inadvertently, and even purposefully, test a Master. You will gain more respect from a slave by staying aware and paying attention to his/her behavior and correcting him/her. Emphasis should be placed on correcting or administering punishment for protocol violations as soon as possible. Punishment gives closure and ensures focus. You probably know that slaves will carry around an event such as displeasing the Master, like baggage. They will beat themselves up forever for a simple mistake. A simple punishment such as popping a rubber band that is always located on the slave's wrist, can help give closure to unintentional protocol violations, and assist the slave in striving to please the Master.

Now, I have been speaking here about protocols in the Master/slave relationship. These philosophies can be transferred into other Dom/sub relationships, and to BDSM or role play scenes. Just to be clear, however, what I am talking about is 24/7, always present, behavioral rules. I do not expect anyone not in My service or collared by me to follow My protocols. Respect is earned, and I believe a person, slave or otherwise has the right to address me however they choose, unless they have given themselves to me in consensual servitude. In addition, there are other areas or terms such as Leather Protocols/etiquette, bar etiquette, and many other areas in which members of relevant communities us the word "protocol." These areas are not what I am referring to when I use the word "protocol." Hopefully someday, members of these communities will come together and create acceptable forms of community protocols/ etiquette that will help us all interact and progress.

This is just a sample of My beliefs and philosophies on protocols. I hope in the near future, to publish My book with this same title. To learn more about me, My leather family, My protocols, and My philosophies please visit My web site at www.MasterTallen. com.

About the Author:

Master Tallen began His journey in the Master/slave lifestyle in late 1997. Starting as a slave, Master Tallen gained experience in varied approaches to BDSM and the Master/slave lifestyle. He has attended functions and presented classes throughout the country. His journey from starting as an owned slave and evolving into a Master/Owner, gave Him opportunities to enjoy numerous perspectives of human nature's interaction with the Master/slave lifestyle. His knowledge and strength are helpful in the education of Masters and slaves alike, to better help them develop their own styles and beliefs in their journey.

Master Tallen joined the Faculty of Master Taino's Training Academy in 2003, and has enjoyed the commitment of attending every day of every Weekend Training session since that time. He currently serves as the Academy's Deputy Director. In November 2006, He relocated back to His native Texas from the Washington, DC area, but has kept His commitment to The Training Academy as well as being a Co-chair for The Master slave Conference in Washington, DC, and serving as the Vice President of the Board of Directors of MTTA Inc., a nonprofit organization committed to education in Dominant/submissive relationships.

The creator of the Master/slave Flag unveiled in 2005, Master Tallen, is the 'Commander' of His Leather Family known as Master Tallen's Leather CORPS. Most recently, Master Tallen was honored with the title of Northeast Master 2008, and is the proud Owner of His slave angela.

Protocols in M/s Households

By Sir Stephen

Let's begin with a question: What makes protocols worth the expenditure of time it takes to create, edit and refine them to the point where they can persist and be of value in an M/s Relationship? In order to explain why, in my opinion, the expenditure of time and effort is well spent, I think it is necessary for me to say a bit about my concept of M/s Relationships and my concept of protocols.

I begin with the terms I will employ in this article – please note that the definitions and usage I present here are not to be misconstrued as universally accepted. They reflect my current understanding, and the general application I make of these terms in my own life and relationships, and are offered solely to provide common ground for purposes of this article.

While it is possible for M/s Households to take many forms, for purposes of this article I will limit my discussion to my experience, which is that of a Household comprised of one Master with one full-time slave and other part-time slaves.

I use the term Master as non-gender specific and in reference to the person who has taken the leadership role in the M/s relationship. The Master assumes the responsibility for creating and maintaining viable policies and procedures designed to give the greatest possible chance of long-term success for the relationship(s) embodied in the Household. Once such policies and procedures are established the Master assumes the responsibility for decision- making on behalf of all involved in service to the Household, in a fashion consistent with the established policies and procedures.

I use the term slave as non-gender specific and in reference to those who have voluntarily sworn obedience to the Master in an M/s relationship. By virtue of their commitment they undertake to act in accordance with the particulars of the Household policies and procedures, and implement the decisions of the Master to the best of their ability.

In my mind M/s relationships are characterized by several key elements:

- First, such relationships are consensual.
- Second, there is a hierarchical structure in place. This structure is based upon a consciously constructed power imbalance which grants one individual (the Master) final authority in decisions for the Household.
- Third, the creation, enforcement, and maintenance of an established set of policies and procedures which might include such items as protocols, rules, rituals, ceremonies, etc.
- Fourth, the persistent application of the policies and procedures (this persistent application is often referred to as being 24/7 in nature). In my opinion this differentiates M/s relationships from other power exchange based relationships in which the power exchange, or the hierarchical structure, exists in support of time-limited activities (often referred to as scenes).
- Finally, successful long-term M/s relationships are characterized by a commitment to that long-term success on the part of all the members of the Household. Such a commitment is demonstrated by the willingness, on the part of all involved, to do the work required to make a success of the Household policies and procedures.

Individual M/s relationships may well incorporate other elements as well, but I think the above lies at the core of such relationships and Households.

What are protocols?

There are various dictionary definitions for the word protocol.

The differences in the definitions revolve around the specific area to which the protocol is applied such as the military, the diplomatic corps, corporate, medical, legal, the scientific community, etc. In general where protocols serve as a tool in facilitating interpersonal relationships (as opposed to, for example, a scientific protocol) they are defined as a preliminary document designed to make it possible for more detailed policies, procedures and agreements to emerge. Thus, Merriam Webster online dictionary defines protocols in the following manner:

"1: an original draft, minute, or record of a document or transaction

2 a: a preliminary memorandum often formulated and signed by diplomatic negotiators as a basis for a final convention or treaty"

Contrary to the working definition of the word some protocols can be quite detailed and quite lengthy. I do not consider mine to be all that detailed, although the current document runs 21 pages, inclusive of a smattering of photographs, and can be found online at www.restraining-order.com

What policies and procedures did I choose to address in my Household protocols?

I felt that I needed to cover the following

- My vision of my Roles and Responsibilities as Master
- My vision of the Roles and Responsibilities for those in service to me
- A Code of Conduct (binding upon both Master and slaves)
- Goals for my Household
- The process for admittance to my Household
- The process for the termination of service
- Speech – tone and manner of speech, rather than specific phrasing (although examples of specific phrasing I find pleasing are included)
- Examples of key rituals

The list above does not cover everything contained with my protocols, so, again, if you are interested in the complete document please feel free to access it on the internet and to use it as a model for your own protocols if you find it to your liking.

I limited the specifics in my protocols as I believe that protocols should not contain elements are likely to change, or if such elements are included there should be caveats attached to them. What do I mean by that? Let's look at rituals. Within my protocols I describe a ritual for greeting me at the door. I specified that such a ritual will exist and that a certain key phrase ("Thank you for allowing me to serve you today, Master") will be spoken. Should the slave also kneel or bow or lie flat on the ground when performing this ritual? I specify in my protocol that the physical action that accompanies the spoken aspect of the ritual will be uniquely defined for each slave. Why?   Well, if you have a ritual specified in your protocols that involves kneeling, how do you accommodate a slave with a knee injury, or just the joint stiffness that accompanies aging? Rather than adjusting and readjusting protocols to the specific and changing needs and limitations of each of the individuals in my service, I attempted to craft my protocols so that they will stand the test of time. Certain rituals are essential and must be carried out on a regular basis. These are enumerated in my protocols but, the physical specifics of such rituals may change based upon varying factors and I personally do not care to re-write my protocols each time I run into some new exception. With that in mind, I manage such specifics external to my protocols.

This is not to say that protocols do not or cannot change – but they should not be subject to frequent minor tinkering. A well written set of protocols provides a basis for the creation of additional, more detailed and specific structural elements, created external to the protocols, as needed.

In the final analysis I believe that protocols provide the broad context in which members of the Household will operate.   This broad context, properly understood, provides greater motivation for everyone in the Household. The Household goals included in my protocols serve to give meaning to the assigned tasks, chores, and responsibilities of all the members of the Household. My slaves inform me that this is a source of comfort to them when I am distracted from my Household responsibilities by other demands in my life. During such times it is the application of the protocols that provides them with a firm footing for their day to day activities and practices.

Giving our work together a purpose; defining unique roles and responsibilities; defining goals; all this, which is in the protocols, promotes greater productivity for the Household in an atmosphere of peace and harmony. This end result – a productive, peaceful, harmonious Household – is what I strive to attain, and I believe that my protocols, in no small measure, contribute to that goal. This makes protocols an extremely useful tool and well worth the effort required to create, modify and maintain them.

About the Author:

Sir Stephen has been actively involved in the BDSM community for over 11 years. He is currently a member of The Eulenspiegel Society (TES), Dom sub Friends (DsF), The National Coalition for Sexual Freedom (NCSF). He is an officer of MasT: Metro NY, and Director and Founder of MAsT: Central NJ. In 2005 he organized and hosted the first Mid-Atlantic Masters' Forum, now an annual event.

He is proud to be the holder of the titles of International Master 2005, and Northeast Master 2004 and has been nominated in both 2006 and 2007 for the Pantheon of Leather Man of the Year Award.

He has presented on numerous occasions, individually, jointly with slave catherine as well as others, and on panels.

PEBRS

Black Tie is not just a rope trick

By Cecelia S.

There was a time, not too long ago, when people understood that the term "Black Tie" meant ultra formal. Although it referred to attire, it really alluded to the full atmosphere of a specific event. Recently, I said that something was "very black tie" and was asked what kind of technique was that kind of tie? Was it like shibari?

I tried to explain that the term referred to a set of formal social protocols – and before I could elaborate, eyes glazed over and interest was gone. Except for a few very vocal people who had to make sure everyone around knew that THEY don't follow any one's protocols and this lifestyle is not about "formal social protocols!"

Of course, they are absolutely correct. The lifestyle – whether you are into BDSM or Leather or DS or Master/slave .. or any of a dozen different variations – is not *about* protocols. Formal or otherwise. However, the protocols are, in my opinion, a necessary and crucial part of the lifestyle.

For the majority of us, when we first started to explore the concept of S/M, we weren't coming in to find formal behaviors and attitudes. We wanted the hot sexy kinky play. Some of us stayed for that. The whole idea of finding others who like what we like, and were not repelled. People who were attracted to pain and hard sex. That worked fine.

So what ARE all these protocols? And why are they important? If it is just about the hot sex, what do we need with Sir and Ma'am and walking one step behind to the left? Or is that to the right? Or in front? And if the protocols are so important, then why are they all different and why can't someone tell me what they ARE! How come there isn't a book that can just spell it out once and for all?

The answer to that question is both simple and complex. The easy answer is that we all do what is right for us. There is no "one true way" or one proscribed protocol that everyone will follow. The more complex answer is that as we came together, we evolved in to groups of friends, clubs, and communities. For groups to survive and grow, the members of the group develop mutually agreed upon ways to interact, and these ways develop into social standards and protocols.

The foundation of what we do is laid with the hot sexual overtones of power exchange. Some give up power. Others take it. Sexual energy permeates every aspect of our society. It is only natural that the social interactions we developed within those parameters would reflect these dynamics.

And yet, even as long as there have been kinky people, there is no one over-arching set of behaviors that define us as a community. The best that anyone came come up with, when talking to a new person, is to "use your company manners" or "your Sunday best manners" that you learned as a child. Behave in a more formal (there's that word again) manner, and soak up what is there.

It begs the question – why the "more formal" manner? Why not just every day politeness? Part of the answer lies in the idea of creating an atmosphere. We aren't gathering together to discuss the weather or look at the animals in the zoo. We are drawn to each other because of that power dynamic that is expressed through S/M, or as some call it BDSM.

A good analogy would perhaps be a renaissance faire. When we arrive, we find there are people who are really taken by the whole idea. They spend large amounts of time, energy and money to create the kind of persona they wish to present. Others are less involved, but still wear costumes. Still others just wear street clothes. But all manage to acquire a manner of speaking and addressing each other that fits into the created atmosphere of the Ren Faire. There is a sense of stepping into another world, if only for a short time.

When new people come in to a munch, in recent years, they have been likely to find very little of that elusive air of "other world" among the people there. Often, the room is crowded and the noise level is incredible, and while there is some flirtation and occasional glimpses of the power dynamic, mostly it feels like the crowd at any mall food court. But then, they go to a meeting or even more incredible, an event. They see Dominants with their submissives, Owners and property. Daddy/boy and Mistress/slaves. Each has their own dynamic. Each has their own protocols of behavior, of modes of address, even of attire. And yet, even though everyone is different, the one common thread that is felt is the sexual dynamic of power exchange. And our formal manners towards each other within this kaleidoscope of relationships is our cultural response of respect for their relationship and a recognition that they are one of us. That WE are all a part of what it is that we do.

We want to be treated with politeness and respect when we are interacting in our community. We offer that level to others, and we frequently receive back what we have given. That is how human societies develop their cultural protocols. Ours is no different. That is why, at a minimum, we use "company manners" when we are among our peers.

That, however, is not the full answer to why we should follow these protocols? Other than the obvious reason that we wish to be a part of the community, what more could there be?

Why do people go to church socials or join bike clubs? For many, it is the same reason we go to lifestyle clubs and events. We not only want to be among people like ourselves, but frequently we are there to look for and attract a partner.

There is a delicate balance that people try to achieve, and sometimes the effort needed to maintain that balance seems to be overwhelming. A dominant who is bossy and arrogant to all who are around does not tend to garner respect from the community at large, but is often tolerated with the belief that the person will eventually self regulate and fit into the community. A dominant who is bossy and arrogant at all times to those perceived to be submissive is likely to find that the submissives in a community will not respond to their overtures. By the same token, people who identify as submissive will not attract a potential dominant if they do not behave in some way that indicates what their nature is. A doormat personality, submissive to any and every potential dominant who walks by, is typically not seen as a potential partner. And yet, behaving in an assertive or aggressive manner also will not serve. It is indeed a precarious line, for both sides.

The most common submissive lament is "Why should I follow any one else's protocol if I am not in a relationship with them?" And from the dominants "I'm the DOM here. I choose my own rules and protocols; I do not follow anyone else's. Like it or lump it."

To steal from a famous TV host... you have to ask , "So, how's that working for you?"

If you are a dominant, why SHOULD you be polite and use your company manners with everyone, including the submissives? Because if they are not YOUR personal submissive, with whom you have an established relationship, then to treat them with anything less than polite respect is not only inappropriate, but will label you as someone who does not understand the basic foundation of our lifestyle, which is one of consent. Until someone has consented to obey you, you have no right to demand anything of them. You are equals.

If you are a submissive, why SHOULD you be polite and use your company manners with everyone, including dominants you do not know or have a relationship with? This one is a little tricky. If you are not in a relationship with that person, all you owe them is the same basic polite respect that we all typically agree is owed to anyone simply because they are human. If you wish for them, or anyone else, to see you as a potential partner, however, you need to convey that you are a submissive, and available. One way to do that is to up the level of formality just a little more. Be aware that just as capping a name online does not make someone a dominant, claiming to be a submissive without any evidence of it won't make people consider you to be a submissive.

It all comes back to the question of "Why should I follow any kind of protocol other than my own?" A question that seems to have no answer, which many people still seem to believe justifies behaving in ways that do not reflect well upon themselves.

But there is an answer. If you are in a relationship, you will have protocols for your own relationship. You naturally expect and desire that those protocols will be respected (if not followed) by those people in the lifestyle whom you associate with. If you wish them to respect your lifestyle choices, you must respect theirs. And together, your interactions with others of like mind, help build the atmosphere and community we all desire to belong to. If you are not in a relationship, but are looking, then by reinforcing the positive protocols and formality that are the hallmark of most of our lifestyle group meetings and events, you will draw the kind of attention from the type of person you are hoping to attract.

Why are you here? If it is just the hot sex, that's fine. If you want to find a partner, that's fine. If you want to just be involved as an active member of the community or simply as a voyeur passing through. All of that is fine. But regardless of your answer, if you make the effort to help enhance the atmosphere, to reinforce the bedrock dynamic of our lifestyle, you will find your own experience that much richer. And protocols are the tools that we use to express that magical reality of consensual power exchange.

About the Author:

Slave Cecelia was introduced to the lifestyle more than 15 years ago in Washington state. Originally a member of the Triskelli Guild, she was active in the greater Seattle area for several years. Cecelia moved to Washington DC in time for BR X (the first ever BR Event.) and was active in Black Rose, Strictly Social, and several other groups in the area. She found her way to Texas in 2000, and was the collared slave of Master David Brown of Fort Worth. Cecelia has been an active member of a number of groups in the DFW area, and has served on the board of several of them. She has also been a long time member of several international organizations. She is a popular presenter, and has given classes and workshops for many groups and events over the years. Currently unowned, Cecelia moved to Houston in 2007, and is becoming an active member in her new local community.

Development of Protocols in the Order for Discipline and Service

By slave elizabeth

When Dr. Bob spoke with me about writing an article on our household's "unusual set of protocols", I must confess that I was slightly taken aback. Truthfully, I could not think of anything that "unusual" about them, let alone think of a reason why anyone would want to read about them. However, upon further reflection, I have come to realize that perhaps the Order for Discipline and Service does have a slightly different viewpoint on how M/s relationships should be arranged.

The ODS protocols are designed to be practical, and encompass the minimum number of rules for the maximum number of circumstances. Our protocols are, for us, logical ways to do things that are sustainable over time. They are what we do everyday, not an act for special occasions. In short, they are a way of organizing our behavior to ensure the reinforcement of the M/s dynamic.

The most visible protocol in ODS is the practice of keeping slaves chained whenever possible (and yes, this includes sleeping.) It is no secret that Mr. McG enjoys metal bondage. The clank of chains and the sight of shiny cuffs at wrists and ankles, are, without a doubt, pleasing to him; however, to say that this protocol developed solely because it is pleasing to him would be attributing very superficial motives to what can be a profoundly moving experience.

There are several different levels of restraints, depending on circumstances. Complete chaining, which would occur at home or at an event, involves the wearing of a collar, wrist and ankle cuffs, and a set of chains connecting the collar to the wrist and ankle cuffs. At other times, slaves are limited to the wearing of collar and cuffs only. This is not as onerous as it sounds. Ankle cuffs are easily hidden by pants and wrist cuffs can be disguised under sweat bands in summer and long-sleeved shirts in winter. The cuffs are a safe way for the slave to stay connected to their slavery when it is not possible to be chained. Only as a last resort (i.e., airport security, work, and visits with biological family) would a slave be without cuffs, and even then they would still keep wearing the chain collar.

The purpose of this protocol is three fold. First, it is pleasing to Mr. McG. He has enjoyed seeing people chained since early childhood. Second, it serves to provide a constant, low-level reminder of one's status, either as master or slave. Being chained helps the slave stay in the right head-space and helps the master to see the slave as a slave, not as a girlfriend/boyfriend. In the past, mistakes were made in not chaining slaves more frequently. If a slave likes to be chained it is a plus, but the slave's enjoyment is beside the point. A slave should never be without some form of restraint, which is why a collar's design should not be able to be confused with a piece of jewelry, nor should it be able to be readily removed. This is particularly important when the master and slave are separated, for then the collar provides a daily visual reminder of the M/s relationship. And lastly, chaining reinforces and helps sustain the countercultural perspective of our non-egalitarian lifestyle. For us, it is as normal for a slave to be chained as it is to have breakfast.

The second protocol related to chaining is the practice of tethering of slaves at night. This involves attaching the slave's collar to a longer piece of chain which is in turn attached to the wall in the slave's cell or to the bed frame in the event that the slave is spending the night in Mr. McG's bedroom or in a hotel. Tethering accomplishes several things. At night we are alone with our thoughts. Being tethered provides the opportunity to have a quiet time of reflection that someone else agrees with your perception that you are a slave. In short, it reinforces the slave's self-identification. Over the years, Mr. McG has determined that, as a whole, slaves are somewhat less secure than the average person and crave guidance and direction. Tethering is a wonderful way for the master to say "You are important to me. I want you here in the morning." Additionally, slaves should not have unlimited freedom. If you could do anything you wanted to as a slave, then what are you submitting to? Tethering limits the slave's ability to exercise initiative, and makes real the notion that the slave's will is secondary to that of the master. Finally, tethering is a protection for a slave. With very few exceptions, every slave that Mr. McG has ever met would do anything to please their master. Tethering at night is a good way to turn the slave "off" and enforce a rest period.

The protocol of slaves having cells evolved in response to having slaves sleeping chained to the walls around the dungeon. The original idea was for bedding to be rolled up during the day. The reality was that slaves staked out their favorite spot and made nests. This had a negative effect, with clothing and bedding scattered around the room. In addition, slaves who snore are annoying to others sharing the same space. Giving each slave an individual space solved these problems. Taken from the Benedictine model, each slave has a modestly sized cell which contains a bed with storage space underneath. Slaves are free to decorate their cells as they wish, as denying individual expression entirely is a bad idea. The cells are a refuge from having to deal with someone else's needs all day, and masters should spend minimal amounts of time in the cells.

Initially, Mr. McG's idea was to lock the slaves in the cells at night and unlock the cells in the morning. However, he quickly determined that there was a major downside to this protocol. In order for him to lock the slaves in at night and let them out again in the morning, he then had to be the last to go to bed and the first to rise. To quote Mr. McG, "This was a bad plan." Ideally, a system would be in place that would automatically lock the cells at night and unlock them in the morning or in the event of an emergency. Lacking this system, the cells are currently kept unlocked at night, and the keys for the tether are kept chained to the wall of the cells so slaves can de-tether in case of emergency. In addition, the wiring has been completed for a "panic button" to be installed in Mr. McGs bedroom. This would sound an alarm in the cells so that the slaves may respond if he has a medical emergency.

There is also another drawback to the slaves sleeping in cells.

As the cells are in the basement and Mr. McG's bedroom is on the second floor, the slaves are not easily accessible to serve his sexual needs at night. This resulted in the practice of slaves sleeping on the floor at the foot of the bed on a rotating basis. All slaves should have the opportunity to sleep in the master's room whether or not they are the master's sexual partner. Furthermore, in a multiple slave household, having sex in the cells will cause jealousy and dissent. Reserving sex for the master's bedroom can alleviate this problem.

The Order for Discipline and Service pioneered the idea of a household uniform protocol. We have uniforms for day, evening, and events, and the uniform is worn by the entire household, master and slave alike. Mr. McG wears the uniform to show that his commitment to the rules of the household is at least equal to what he expects of his slaves. He developed this protocol as a way to ensure household harmony. Slaves come in various shapes and sizes. Dressing them in the same manner eliminates any sort of competition among them as to who has the more attractive wardrobe.

The uniforms we wear the most are the casual day uniform and the evening uniform. The casual day uniform consists of a polo shirt bearing the ODS insignia, black jeans, and black sneakers or boots. This uniform is appropriate for most day-to-day activities around the house and can be worn while grocery shopping, etc. Depending upon circumstances, it can even be worn to one's job. The evening uniform consists of a set of black hospital scrubs. Having a distinct evening uniform serves the purpose of re-directing the slave's attention. Putting on the evening uniform means the day's work is done, and visually distinguishes the work day from the non-work day.

There are two additional uniforms: a formal dress uniform and an event uniform. The formal uniform consists of a light blue oxford shirt with the ODS monogram on the left pocket, navy blue slacks with belt, and black shoes. This is worn when accompanying the master to business related functions, or when acting as chauffeur. The event uniform consists of a black polo shirt with the ODS insignia on the left, black jeans, and black sneakers or boots. However, while at a dungeon or play party, slaves may wear their attire of choice, be it latex, PVC, or a corset.

We also have protocols for appearance. Slaves are required to maintain a short haircut as an act of submission to the master's will. (This is a wonderful way to ascertain if a candidate for the household will work out, depending on whether or not they are willing to cut their hair as part of the application process.) In addition, female slaves do not wear makeup or perfume. Again, this has a two-fold purpose. Mr. McG prefers his slaves to have an androgynous appearance, and not wearing makeup or having a fussy hairstyle greatly facilitates the speed with which slaves can be ready to leave the house.

I have saved our most unusual protocol for last. In our household, slaves are not required to call Mr. McG "Master". "Master" is an important title. To refer to someone as "Master" means they have achieved a high level of acumen in some area. One cannot bestow the title of "Master" on oneself. It is the slave who is in the best position to determine if their owner has mastered the art of command. The slave should not be pressured into calling his or her owner "Master". "Sir" is the appropriate honorific to distinguish the owner from the owned.

Mastery should not be an exercise in egotism. Owners who are afraid to be judged by those whom they command are inherently unworthy of that command.

About the Author:
Jack McG

Jack is a het, male, dominant with a passion for bondage and a long-held interest in the dynamics of M/s relationships. He is a founding member of Black Rose, an emeritus member of its board of directors, and the current President. Previously he served Black Rose in several capacities including Chairman of the Board, President, Secretary and Co-chair for BR10. Additionally, he serves as Chairman of the Board of CARAS (Community-Academic Consortium for Research on Alternative Sexualities). Further, he serves as Vice-Chairman of the Board of MTTA, Inc., a not-for-profit corporation that owns Master Taino's Training Academy, the annual Master/slave Conference and MAsT Washington, DC. He is also an emeritus member of the LLC, Inc. board and served as its Vice-Chairman and Treasurer as well as Co-chair for LLC2000. Jack was the first Chairman of the Board of NCSF.

slave elizabeth
slave elizabeth met Mr. McG on Nov. 23, 2002, and thought

he was nice guy with whom she had interests in common. She was collared on Nov. 23, 2003.

Protocols in M/s Relationships: Origin, Usage, and Development

By Eric Pride

A recent meeting and discussion at the Metro New York chapter of MAsT (Masters And slaves Together) on protocols and rituals in M/s relationships got me inspired to write this essay. Thank you all for a great meeting!

Some M/s relationships have protocols, others do not. Some think protocols make their relationship different and unique, others mean that they are too complex and make their relationships inflexible and rigid. In this essay I will discuss the origin of protocols in the M/s community, their usage and applicability, and some ways of how they can be developed and structured. I will also try to convey some of the benefits and rewards that M/s relationships using protocols experience.

Note that this document is written using certain deferential capitalization and spelling not uncommon in the M/s lifestyle. Furthermore, I use "Master/He" to refer to the dominant person or persons, and "slave/she" to the submissive person or persons in the relationship. This is for matters of convenience only.

The Merriam-Webster's dictionary defines a protocol to be "a code prescribing strict adherence to correct etiquette and precedence (as in diplomatic exchange and in the military services)". In other words, a protocol is a set of rules and conventions to be followed in interaction and communication between, for example, peers, superiors, and subordinates. It might specify anything from how the slave should perform certain tasks or actions, how she should speak at home or in public, to how she should dress and behave at formal tea service. Potentially, it could contain anything and everything the Master wants.

Most people seem to agree with that the usage of protocols in the scene dates back to the "Old Guard". Gay World War II veterans returning back home formed groups that applied a structure similar to the one that they had been exposed to during the war. Each group had their own set of secret rules that members had to strictly follow. In many cases, the rules were developed into formal protocols sometimes also including rituals such as newcomer initiations and slave collarings. These rules and protocols, whether simple or complex, created a secret code among the initiated that over time developed a strong group feeling and unity between the members. The protocols gave them a simple way of distinguishing themselves from others thereby establishing a clear separation between "we" and "them".

The features of the military mindset from the "Old Guard" stayed and got incorporated into the scene in general. Today, without being "Old Guard", many M/s practitioners use protocols in their relationships. Often these protocols are relationship specific and have been developed over time among the people involved. So why are protocols used in these relationships? There are as many answers to this question as there are people using protocols. However, the most common reasons appear to be that the protocol:

- creates a clear distinction between the Master and the slave
- provides a good foundation for the relationship
- through its rules clarifies for the slave how to serve and behave in different situations
- strengthens the bond between Master and slave by distinguishing them and their unique relationship from others

Most protocols are directed towards the slave. They often regulate the slave's behavior, communication, and interaction in one way or the other. Protocols can be very simple or very detailed. They can prescribe the specific way in which certain tasks have to be performed. The slave might have to use specific honorifics and figures of speech for addressing her Master. Each individual task or action might have its own rules. Clearly, the more specialized the rules are, the more difficult they become to learn as well as to enforce. When the number of rules increases (and often it does if one tries to provide rules for every possible situation) the protocol becomes cumbersome and almost impossible to keep track of. The slave will have difficulty learning and separating the numerous rules for all the different situations. It will also become very difficult for the Master to reinforce and correct all mistakes.

Many practitioners agree that protocols should be simple and to the point. They should enforce a certain general behavior and obedience which can be extrapolated and applied to many types of situations. The rules provide a foundation for the M/s relationship and enforce a certain dynamics between the Owner and the property. Simplicity, generality and broad applicability go a long way.

Let us take a look at some of the typical components of a protocol. Obviously, each Master has His ways of having things done, and this exposé is slightly biased towards our own views.

General behavior

The slave lives to please and serve her Owner under any circumstance and at any time. This implies that the slave should always focus on her Master -- His safety, needs, and desires. she should put Him first in any situation as long as that does not put the slave into any danger. The slave should never show any sign of anger or frustration, crankiness or any disruptive behaviors, emotions or thoughts. she should never show any disagreement with an order or wish from her Owner. All orders should be promptly complied with and diligently executed.

Many Masters are concerned about their slave's general appearance and therefore include requirements thereof in the protocol. For example, the slave might have to comply to certain hygiene requirements and only be allowed to wear certain approved clothing. General eating or weight restrictions are also common.

Communication

In general, the slave is always expected to speak and express herself in a respectful manner, whether she is talking to her Master or anyone else. Often a slave is required to use proper honorifics in the presence of her Master and other people involved in the scene. The slave might be required to refer to her Master as "Master", "Sir", "my Master" or "my Owner", and herself in third person such as "slave", "this slave", "Your property" or simply "she/he/it". It is also common that the slave has to ask her Master's permission before beginning any activity. For example, instead of the slave saying, "I am going to the restroom" she would be required to express this basic need as a request and use proper honorifics -- "Sir, would it please Master if slave went to the restroom to take care of herself, Sir?"

Interaction

When entering into the awareness of her Master a slave might be required to announce her presence by a simple curtsy or present. This present serves to acknowledge the slave's status and readiness to provide any services her Master may require. Depending on the situation or the location the slave might present either kneeling or standing.

For an Owner, it is practical in public situations to always know where your slave is. Having the slave on one preassigned side simplifies fetching, carrying, or any other type of attending service she provides. It also minimizes bumping into each other while walking or just standing around.

Variations

As pointed out above, there are many variations to protocols. Every Master has his own way of doing things. Some Masters use different protocols in different situations. A protocol can be location or situation dependent, i.e. depending on where the slave is or who the slave is interacting with, different rules may apply. In public places some of the more formal rules may be changed. Speech patterns using "Sir" or "Master" might be less restrictive in public in order to not draw attention from the surrounding. Similarly, the present might be performed in a different way in public situations. For example, a full kneeling present could be substituted by a subtle head bow accompanied by lowering of the eyes. With some thought and ingenuity it is possible to still maintain a certain protocol even in public. Clearly, it will be less formal (unless you want to get the attention of bypassers - or shock them!) but still a protocol is in place enforcing proper M/s dynamics.

A protocol provides a good way to set a minimum standard for a slave's behavior, communication, and interaction. Start your protocol from a few simple rules. It is hard to construct a complete or full-blown protocol right away. You and your slave will need time to accommodate new rules and structures, so the simpler the better. Over time, modifications and more details can be added. Using an existing protocol developed by someone else for inspiration is also very helpful.

Make sure that rules and specific positions or tasks are thoroughly understood. Practice them together, make adjustments, and correct mistakes when they occur. This is often referred to as "protocol training" or just "training". In the early stages, before the slave is proficient with the protocol, it might be very tiresome to correct each and every error. But if this is not done, you will achieve poor results. In the beginning, it is important to review the protocol on a regular basis together. Like anything else in an M/s relationship, if your slave is not doing something the way you want it or to your liking, you have to change it. After a while, the slave will start correcting herself and taking great pride in staying in protocol and following the rules. Keep in mind that a protocol is never static. It will evolve and change over time as you and your household become more comfortable with it.

Besides knowing how the slave will behave and perform in different situations, the protocol can be an important spiritual part of the M/s relationship. For many it is something that becomes very personal and intimate, sometimes providing a strong symbol for the household.

A protocol is not developed overnight. It takes time and hands-on experience to build and put into effect. Although the real results might not become apparent until after long time use, it is a well spent effort. You and your household will have something unique.

About the Author:

Sir Eric heads, together with his wife Lady Christie, an M/s based household in New York City. The primary focus of The Pride Household is toward integrating healthy power-exchange dynamics into daily life, and to provide guidance, training, and support for its individual servants and slaves. He enjoys consensual SM and control, has published several thought-provoking essays on different aspects of structured lifestyles, and is an active member of MAsT (Metro New York), TES, and NCSF. Along with other members of his household, he is a regularly invited moderator and speaker at leather and lifestyle organizations, including among others the Master/slave Conference and the Mid-Atlantic Masters' Forum. Sir Eric is also a principal organizer of the forthcoming Master slave Development Center (MsDC). He can be reached at Eric_Pride@yahoo.com.

Bornslaves:
Protocol, Concept and Reality

by SlaveMaster

For almost 15 years I pursued the Master/slave fantasy described by the best erotic fiction available. There was enough truth written in those stimulating pages for me to believe what I read. The result was two long-term conventional Master/slave relationships. Each came to an end after investing six years in one, eight in the other.

I had developed tremendous power and control but had exhausted my ability to direct it. The relationships ultimately ended because I felt as though I was driving a powerful sports car through a dark tunnel without any lights. I didn't know where to steer, so I couldn't determine what orders to issue to fulfill my responsibilities to the slaves.

A series of events surrounding what I call my "defining moment" caused me to promise to never believe in anything I wasn't willing to live by, and to never live by anything I didn't believe. Previously, I found it both entertaining and comforting to eloquently defend a variety of positions. I loved arguing for argument's sake. Winning an argument, however, didn't make the argued principles true, much less something by which anyone could live.

The long series of events that changed my life put me back in contact with a long time friend and motorcycle buddy who had taken his own slave. I knew my purpose now was different from the traditional "Master" role I'd always taken. If not "Master," what was my relationship to a slave? At 3:00 one early morning I fitfully awoke. The answer to who I am came suddenly and surely, "SlaveMaster." Both my name and role were given in that moment. A spiritual name over which I had no choice and no right of refusal was handed to me. I tried ignoring the use of the assigned name, but life stops working well for me whenever I try to pretend this isn't who I am.

Simultaneous with my new spiritual confidence to "guide a powerful sports car through a dark tunnel" came an invitation from my friend, the Master, to help build and deepen his relationship with his slave. For the first time, my own personal obedience to do whatever I was given to do freed me to accept responsibilities for slave creatures that I wasn't egotistically qualified for. A lack of knowledge of the future no longer held me back from doing what needed to be done. Previously, I thought my qualification depended upon having an intricate and immediate understanding of all the nuances of human nature. I found it both humbling and a relief to know differently.

Now I feel emboldened and confident to develop and require a slave's absolute and complete obedience. There is no fear of exhausting the constant guidance that I need personally, nor of running out of that which I pass on to my slaves as orders. I consider obedience received from a slave to be a gift. The quantity of that gift is always matched by my responsibility taken. The equality of this exchange is an unbreakable personal commitment that supplements my personal vow to always act in the best interest of any slave to whom I issue orders.

I began work with my friend's slave one afternoon or evening at a time. The techniques I used were not a lot different from those employed before my spiritual clarity. My intention, however, was now different. Flogging is my favorite form of physical SM and over time has proved to be the most effective at producing the spiritual effects that result from a slave-development intention. Without the fears and constraints of human knowledge I was able to explore my newly developing slave. It became a wild adventure into the unknown.

The slave's reactions during development ranged from uncontrollable laughter to the visualization of angels that spoke naturally with the slave. The angel vision was so real that the developing slave could not believe that it wasn't both visible and audible to me as well. The profound benefit of the angel's presence was dialogue and insight into spiritual events that I could never have otherwise discovered. I combined the slave's expressed experiences with mine, and added that to what I knew from 15-years experience and what the angel expressed that was passed onto me by the slave.

I conducted each session with the purpose of taking the development as far as it would go. The slave was more than willing. The Master's personal support and presence provided a security and connection that reduced the developing slave's fear and reluctance to go into the unknown. The joy of the adventure overshadowed any fears or hesitation either of us felt.

The slave invited every experience. Most couldn't be explained with words, almost none could be understood with psychological principles, and none could be denied due to the power of the experience. The more strange and less expected the slave's reactions were, the more significant was each accumulating result.

Specifically, each important life event was revisited, going all the way back to the first memories of childhood. All hesitations to "go there" were overcome by the unfailing insistence of the flogger, which by its very nature demands staying in the present and facing what is coming next.

When revisited, childhood, adolescent, and even adult experiences were suddenly viewed from the perspective of how each experience contributed to the slave's life in a positive way. It even became clear that every event was necessary to produce each significant subsequent event that defined the slave's life. This forced the slave to recognize that especially the experiences that were viewed as negative at the time were, in fact, critical and essential.

Everything that made the slave passionate, all that the slave cared about, the most deeply held principles, and even the professional work pursued, had been defined by what had to have happened, exactly as it did. A lot of tears and regret, fears, and huge amounts of grieving bubbled up from my floggings, offered with no intention except for giving love and power. Through practice I learned how to prevent contaminating the slave development process with my own agenda or personal intention.

Many modern and classical spiritualists have described the requirement of re-contextualizing life to enter spiritual adulthood. When I abandoned my egotistic flogging intentions and stopped trying to control the outcome, both the impact and the diversity of the resulting experiences multiplied many times over. The process took on a purpose and meaning beyond my comprehension or control.

Session after session resulted in experience after experience. So much happened that I was tempted to think that this could be used as a substitute for therapy. Only years later did I learn the distinction between spiritual evolution and the science of therapy. I discovered that the development didn't work at all when I tried to take credit for what was accomplished, or when I attempted to duplicate some previous action or process that had worked before. The only time anything "worked" at all was when I followed my heart, beyond understanding. This confirmed both my own spirituality and the clear and legitimate alternative purpose for flogging, or any other form of physical SM that involved the delivery of power.

I had a growing feeling of being out of control as the slave development became increasingly effective. Sometimes it took days for the slave to feel "normal" again, while what had happened settled in and the insights and growth became conscious. Occasionally, flu-like symptoms would appear for 24 hours at a time. At other times, nausea and other body reactions appeared. The slave met the challenge of finding the additional courage and motivation increasingly needed to overcome all the doubts and unknowns that appeared as a result of what happened each previous time. I'm clear why most don't accept their slavery. None of this "just happens." The slave has to want slavery, profoundly, to accept and invite what is necessary for growth and development.

Over time, the slave developed a growing need for something specific to happen. There was even a tendency for us jointly to develop anticipation for a specific, but unknown, event to occur. Specific goals were abandoned, but the need for some benchmark grew, and the more elusive any conclusion became. Part of the time I felt like a dog chasing its tail. I didn't know what I wanted to happen, but I felt a need for something.

Almost frantically, I scheduled more and more sessions. The time I wanted to spend developing the slave began to compete for the slave's time with his Master — they had a long-term relationship.

I had an exhausted feeling, but it wasn't as strong as the slave's.

In a feeling of concession, the slave decided that surrendering to additional development was worthwhile even if we couldn't accomplish any particular objective. We both felt relief and an emotional sigh as we released ourselves from the overwhelming responsibility for results. Our conclusion that pursuit for a reason was futile was, in retrospect, a pivotal decision.

The sessions which followed felt to both of us as though they always ended with the slave on the verge of something. Time after time, a power, a moment, or a pause would appear while high energy was present. Then, repeatedly, a feeling of missed opportunity displaced the anticipation. We tried more energy, longer sessions, different times of day, and scheduled different times in our work week. Nothing seemed to make any difference while the sense of imminence and failure repeated.

Protocol was being formalized between the Master and me, and the slave and me, as well as between the Master and his slave. We hadn't, however, considered changing the self-references the slave used. I decided, finally, to specifically address our being stuck. The slave was clear when the question was presented. "I've been lying!" was the immediate response. The slave went on to explain that the feeling was like one of standing next to someone else's car, claiming it to be his own. That same sense arose each time we approached conclusion.

The current protocol allowed the use of "I," "me," and "my." When any of these self references were used, even silently, during the flogging experiences, the strangeness and overwhelming sense of dishonesty stopped whatever was developing. Without being consciously aware that we were in pursuit of a spiritual process, we discovered that the spirit needs its own language that reflects the truth of its own nature. Forced to compete with conventional language the spirit instantly retreated, leaving us to our human conditions and processes.

The solution was clear. I changed the protocol to disallow the egotistic self references. The primary reference became "this slave." At the time, the change was made to "he" for secondary reference. Later that was replaced with "it" to accurately reflect the absence of gender and the personal, and separate, reference that "he" or "she" implied.

Slave development was suspended for several days while the protocol was practiced and enforced. I later learned that virtually every spiritual development practice speaks to separating who we are from the egotistic masks we define ourselves with. This was a first-hand experience of the crippling effects of maintaining our egos. We both knew how important our discovery was and the new language soon became automatic. Our willingness to make drastic changes came easily from having learned that what is really important is never what we expect it to be. The last hurdle to growth had been discovered.

With the revised protocol in place, an additional session was arranged on a sunny Saturday afternoon. The Master was absent because of a professional commitment. Objectively, the flogging that day was probably performed with less physical energy than usual. That session, however, might have held a greater sense of perseverance since it was conducted with no concern for the outcome. The expectations had disappeared so it was OK just to keep going to see where it would lead. I decided just to relax and have fun.

When this defining session began, each strike caused a visible and deepening surrender in the slave. As was the normal practice, I had the slave bound. The slave developed deep, rhythmic breathing. Like a bellows pumping up, the slave began to force primal, guttural sounds with each exhale. In a growling, territorial call, the body tightened and held against each of the restraints. The howling and pulling continued while I insistently continued to empower the experience with my flogger.

Without a long history of experience that had taught me to ignore reactions and, instead, to continue what I was given to do, I would have backed off, and abandoned the process. What I knew was the body's movements had nothing to do with the spirit's needs. I also couldn't have conducted this session without the confidence and understanding that I had acquired during this particular slave's evolution.

Encouraged to continue by my new-found confidence, the slave started expressing fits of emotion with accompanying body reactions. From moment to moment something different happened. My only challenge was to strike where I intended to strike because of the rapid and unpredictable body movement. Lots of time passed.

Then, like trying to both emotionally and physically shed its shell, with the sounds of fear and anguish, and struggle and attack, the slave fell into a satisfied quiet without notable breathing or movement. I continued flogging, but what I did, or how the flogging changed, caused no reaction. The flogging was over. I brought it to a systematic close.

From having witnessed several childbirths, I recognized the pattern as the same. Birth has pushing and struggle, motivated by desire, that concludes in satisfied relief. This felt the same as when a child first enters the world. It was clear this was "slave BIRTH" and the resulting creature a "BORNSLAVE."

Soon after that time, the slave graduated in its formal field of study and auditioned for the state's largest opera. The result was its acceptance as the youngest to ever be admitted. When questioned why the slave was selected over so many other veteran singers, the slave expressed that when it sang the words to classic music it could feel and therefore express the associated emotion it had experienced during slave development.

BIRTH was the only way I could describe what happened. The sounds and physical reactions were birth. A new life was formed from all the "gestation" that came before, starting with the slave's physical birth. A new acceptance of spirituality as being real, and the physical world as what is only theoretical, was born out of the process.

Neither theology, psychology, physics, nor chemistry can explain what happened then, and has happened to six additional slaves since that first time. Prior experience has taught me that what will happen with the next slave (or with the next flogging session) is that what has happened before is the least likely to happen again. I've learned that having any human intention retards or stops the evolution toward BIRTH. I know now that despite the need for a slave's burning desire to be slave, the desire for any specific outcome, like BIRTH, prevents the event, like a deep, life irony. I've also concluded that *magic* better describes what happens than do any of the sciences.

Equally as profound, and significant to the process, is the need for a new language. Over and over, when the BIRTH moment might have otherwise occurred, human thinking, with the use of "I" and "me" and "my," stopped everything dead in its tracks. Spiritual evolution, above all, requires honesty and when the language we use is not honest, the spirit passively protests by disappearing. Even a subconscious sense of dishonesty instantly rips the mood and the possibilities away.

The natural result of this effort and intention is a protocol which prohibits the use of the usual self references. That protocol is documented at www.bornslaves.com/principles.html and is the language that reflects the reality of the slave mind and spirit. Who knew the spirit needed its own language? When the mind is trained to reflect the truth, the spirit feels at home and has a way to express itself. When our thinking is trained to support reality instead of trying to conform to a false, manufactured human construct, the natural and normal process of spiritual BIRTH occurs.

Few are born to be slaves. I'm convinced that for those lucky few, the real and legitimate process of evolution and growth is the most explicit and direct found on earth. Protocol supports and allows what is designed into a slave to be expressed. The reward is happiness, and there can be no greater return on our investment of life.

Protocols

By Obsidian

The stone dropped into the brown paper bag with a solid 'thunk'. Every time. I peered over the edge of the bag to look inside, confident that I would see a heavy river rock shiny with age and wear. I wondered why something so heavy wouldn't just tear through the paper bag and spill out onto the floor of my grandmother's living room. My uncle Tracy smiled at me and turned the bag over – there was nothing inside apparently. To my seven year old eyes, it was a miracle – one repeated again and again to my amazement. He'd hold the bag in one hand and with a flourish, "drop" an invisible stone inside again and again. Holding my breath, I heard and 'saw' this stone drop in the bag over and over again. I never forgot that magical moment – that was almost 40 years ago. What you may ask has this little narrative to do with protocol? Everything. Nothing. It depends.

Why protocols?

First – what is a protocol? The dictionary offers this definition;

- The forms of ceremony and etiquette observed by diplomats and heads of state.
- A code of correct conduct: safety protocols; academic protocol.

So a set of protocols between Master and slave can be said to be basically a "code of correct conduct." How do protocols differ from rituals? Rituals can be a body of ceremonial acts, or a series of such acts – even a detailed method of procedure, so there may be some overlap between protocol and ritual.

The American Standard Dictionary offers the below;

- A ceremonial act or a series of such acts.
- The performance of such acts.
- A detailed method of procedure faithfully or regularly followed: *My household chores have become a morning ritual.*
- A state or condition characterized by the presence of established procedure or routine.

So as a working definition I like to use this: A protocol is a way of doing something – a standard procedure. Protocol is a form of correct conduct or ceremony or etiquette. A *ritual* is what happens when we take protocol and incorporate our Spirit and intention to elevate protocol to Art. In ritual there is a spiritual component added to the actions taken, an air of contemplation, of ceremony. There is a satisfaction and a comfort taken by the participants in a ritual that connects the participants to something greater than themselves, e.g. slavery or Mastery, the community at large, Spirit or the Divine etc...

Ok, so if we have definitions for protocol and for ritual...what then is a tradition? Protocol for our purposes between Master and slave involves a one-on-one relationship. (e.g. when serving always kneel, kiss the edge of the cup or plate prior to setting the item before Me). Ritual would therefore involve the art of the presentation. How does one kneel when serving? Is it possible to serve perfectly each time? There are a million ways to position your body when serving a cup or plate – which is the most aesthetically pleasing? Which position elevates the activity to something approaching perfection? Over the years we have been together, My slave and I have both discovered a love and appreciation of our own M/s protocol. While it can be a very public, vulnerable and beautiful expression of our relationship it is also can be an intensely private language of the heart that only the two of us are aware of.

My first experience with protocol reminded me of that trick my uncle performed many years ago. Recently I felt that same feeling again, watching friends of ours - some of their protocols touched me very deeply. I remember experiencing what I was watching at a gut level - there was something about it that just dropped into me like that invisible stone and settled there - a *resonance* or more specifically a deep sense of 'rightness' or appropriateness that stayed with me. **Resonance** is critical to establishing protocols that last. While it may be tempting to establish a multitude of very complicated protocols for your slave to begin following, our experience has been that both Master and slave will quickly tire of protocol just for protocols sake. The most appropriate and beautiful protocols that you will create and keep will be those that resonate with you. It will take time, and some trial and error - but with diligence and patience you will discover something very rich and rewarding, and potentially uncover a new depth to your M/s dynamic.

Repeatable and Practical

Questions from the participants in a recent seminar that my slave and I taught on protocol indicated to us that many in the lifestyle are really searching for ideas - the question asked most often is "Where do we start?"

For us, the answer was very simple - at the beginning. Each day presents itself to us as a new unique set of opportunities and circumstances, yet there are broad similarities in the rituals we all perform everyday. We are largely unconscious of the role of ritual in our daily lives - take a moment and consider what you always do without fail each morning? What comes first? There is a sequence of events that feel 'right' to you? - and once you go through that exercise you are ready to start your day. When something interrupts or derails that process it can be difficult to feel comfortable. You go into the day somewhat off-balance. Protocol between Master and slave performs a similar function.

When my slave awakens in the morning, what actions can she perform at my direction that will reaffirm her bond to me as well as reinforce her internal recognition that she is Mine? It helps if the Master divides the day up in thirds. What are the morning rituals that she commonly performs? How would you like things done instead? What matters to you a lot? What items are insignificant? While Im not particularly interested in how she brushes her teeth in the morning, I do have an interest in how she is dressed to go out into the world. In my work I travel quite a bit - when I am traveling on business she is to contact me each morning for my approval of her dress for the day. Why is this significant? Namaste is perfectly capable of selecting something wonderful and appropriate to wear to work each day without my guidance or input. My creation of this protocol has nothing to do with my confidence in her abilities, nor should it be taken as a commentary on her skills in this area. What this protocol does is that it elevates and changes the mundane (*I'm getting dressed for work*) to the important specific activity that reinforces our bond and reestablishes our M/s dynamic (*I'm getting dressed for Master, in something that pleases Him*)

More examples of practical, repeatable protocols:

- When serving food or drink, kneel next to My place at the table, briefly kiss the rim of the cup or plate and then place it before Me.
- Before sitting down at table, pause for a moment and wait for Me to instruct you to take your seat.
- My slave girl must remember that she is property, and should not refer to herself as "I," "me," or to objects as "my" or "mine" in my presence. She instead should say "this girl," "your slave," and similar phrases.

Instructional Protocols

Although most protocols are by their very nature instructional, from time to time in our experience we have had periods in which there are very specific areas of her life and/or activities that require focused, concentrated attention. It is generally accepted that any activity must be performed for 21 days in order to become a habit. The requirement to follow protocols such as these may not be long-term in nature and may be withdrawn once the specific goal has been reached.

My slave is required to know how to dance for me. I will provide instruction as to the type of dance I wish her to learn or perform, and she will then dance as directed by me.

She must take care of her physical body to the best of her ability – this includes pursuing good nutrition, eating three meals a day at minimum, taking her vitamins or nutritional supplements every day and drinking at least 32oz of water during the regular workday

She will not have and/or show a 'negative attitude' in her Master's presence, showing her displeasure with His decisions and/

or command by changing her position, scowling, folding her arms, putting her hands on my hips or making irritated sounds, motions or facial expressions.

Desire, not Deterrence

When we first began exploring protocol and establishing its importance in our relationship, it was very tempting to create a lot of rules and expectations focused on what I didn't want. I actually tried this and it sucked big time. In the protocols I've listed in this article there are some that appear to be more expectation of a particular attitude than instruction to actually do something, and others still that are definitely of the Do Not Do This variety. Im not advocating trying to categorically avoid protocols that focus on the negative – I do however believe Masters can get better results by having a balanced approach. My advice is to start simply – focus on the things that you do want. How do you identify those actions? Have the slave create a list of things that he or she does everyday. When you review the list, ask yourself; Is there anything here that resonates with me?. Look for the practical and repeatable actions. What can you focus on that will deepen their slavery? Later on you can focus on instruction, but for this first time just focus on the practical and everyday. Speech patterns, clothing – how food is prepared and served are good places to begin. Have fun with it and don't take yourself too seriously. Mistakes will be made and I cannot stress strongly enough that you should feel free to discard protocols that do not work for you. May you each find what you are seeking.

About the Author:

Master Obsidian has been involved with the scene for over two decades. He has a passion for diversity and authenticity in relationships and the health and growth of the kink community. Obsidian is the chapter founder and Director of MAsT Austin . He has also served on the Board of GWNN (the Group with No Name) in Austin Texas and has served as moderator of Black BEAT Texas , a lifestyle gateway group for people of color for the past 5 years. Additionally, he and his devoted slave namaste serve as moderators for the national MAsT Open yahoo group as well as the regional MAsT Austin discussion list. He is the author of a number of articles covering the BDSM lifestyle and often serves as a presenter and discussion group facilitator. In addition to seminars and BDSM demonstrations for a number of clubs and organizations, his educational experience also includes workshop presentations and numerous online classes focusing on M/s relationship dynamics. He has also served as mentor to novice Dominants new to BDSM/Leather. He is the owner of slave namaste and the Master of House Obsidian in Austin Texas where they reside when they aren't running around the country working or attending lifestyle events.

Rituals, from the slave's Perspective

By Tala Thera

The first time I knelt in his living room I knew everything would change as he counted the little ways I would show submission from this moment forward.

The first time I kissed his hand and showed gratitude for being allowed to come to him I knew the value of the act.

As my submission deepened, so has the value of these and other little actions. Sir told me that first evening that these actions and rituals would help me set and maintain my headspace.

As the days have grown into months I find myself grateful for those moments when I am reminded of what and who I am.

My favorite is to kneel at the foot of his bed, nude, slave open, waiting for him. Every night I feel a moment of gratitude as he allows me to undress him, after he has gotten comfortably in bed to join him.

One night he went to bed prior to me as I took care of a few last minute chores. He was undressed and covered as I entered the room. As I began to drop to my knees, he spoke the words "Come to bed, lil girl." I felt an immediate emptiness, an odd note in the rhythm of my day. As I curled against him and thanked him for allowing me in his bed, I berated myself. You are still in his bed, what is the matter with you? Why are you turning this into a big deal? Why did skipping this ritual, even once, matter?

I returned to the simplest of answers; the one he gave me on that first day. Rituals help set and maintain the headspace of a slave or submissive. I mentioned it the next day to him, and he smiled and said, "I had no idea it meant so much to you. I will remember that in the future."

Sometimes it is an oversight or time constraints that affects the ability to use and perform rituals. Other times it is a change in your schedule that can cause this change and force the couple to find new rituals.

In Metro Detroit, there are many auto workers, so working different shifts is possible. From day shift to midnights and back again upsets the ability to practice your daily routine.

This can have a profound affect on the dynamic. It is not that the hold is so tenuous but that the connections are so important. When the partners may not see each other for days at a time there becomes a sense of disconnections. This can even cause tensions in vanilla relationships.

The important thing is to first recognize there is a problem occurring. This can be challenging, as it is a rare person who recognizes immediately what the problem is. It is possible that the slave is feeling irritable, restless, lonely, displaced, or any of these emotions. We as humans rarely say, "I feel_____" and "I need_____". Even in today's society of self-help it is a challenge. Instead we direct the emotion into what Laura Doyle calls the "red herring."

It can be that Master left his socks on the floor again! Or that tasks have fallen to the slave that were not hers before and she feels overwhelmed. She snaps at the Master or in general, begins to test the limits of her box or withdraws within herself. She places the focus squarely on the perceived burden and magnifies it, acts out against it. In truth she misses her Master, misses the routine, or simply his touch.

It is a wise Master that recognizes the problem or a courageous slave who brings it to his attention. Then the question rises, what do we do to resolve this problem?

There is a simple answer: Create new rituals. When living together but working separate shifts some examples can be: If he likes to shower when he first gets home, lay out his robe, a warmed towel, turn down the blankets, fluff the pillows on the bed.

When you are in the same house personal touches are better.

60

Instead of a computer journal keep a handwritten one, or ask her to write out a fantasy. Then write a comment. "Sounds wonderful!" can have so much value.

Chore lists maintain the control without the physical person and can have much the same effect. As she completes the tasks have her check them off. When you're checking them write on it, "Good Girl" or "redo the stove. Any feedback will have a positive result.

The idea is to reinforce the dynamic ; whether it's online journaling or sticky notes, keep the communications personal.

If a daily ritual such as bedtime is forgotten, journal about it, ask to speak freely about it. The Master or submissive/slave may not know the importance until its not there.

I did not know how much I valued kissing his hand upon entering his home until it was not possible due to houseguests — houseguests that stayed three months! We never truly returned to that routine and I still miss it. Yet I value the other rituals that we still have and I am grateful to him for recognizing their importance.

In power dynamic and vanilla relationships we create rituals. They give us comfort, help us maintain connections and create headspace. The loss of them can be disconcerting and shake the basis of the relationship. Through recognizing the problem and creating new or replacement rituals, we can find a new equilibrium.

About the Author:

Tala Thera is a work in progress, and believes in constant growth through learning and writing is one way to grow, learn and share. She is a submissive who serves MasterGrizly. She entered the local BDSM community as a top/switch some ten years ago. Currently she assists MasterGrizly in the operation of Detroit Space and also runs a "Submissive Ladies Night out Munch" in the area.

PEBRS

My S.O.P.

By Sergeant Major

This may seem a strange title for an article on protocols but, in fact, the use of protocols, conventions and rituals is a form of standard operating procedure. While the term has military overtones, the concept exists in all organizations and groups regardless of the title the specific document may have. The degree of structure and formality varies but even if only an oral tradition it will have meaning and substance for those who are under its influence.

The content serves several purposes, from setting out a philosophy for the organization to establishing a code of conduct to ensure the best possible image. Since each power exchanged based relationship is different and certainly not standard, for this article I will substitute *selection of protocols* for the regular meaning of SOP.

All of us have some form of conventions and protocols we follow in our daily lives. In this article I am presenting those which contribute to my domination and submission based relationships. As the master of a household my SOP is designed to fulfill the five tenets of my philosophy and obligations as a master. The five tenets are to cherish, respect and protect, to lead and to guide. Anyone who petitions to enter my service is a complete person, totally capable of functioning and surviving on their own without me. I do not see my role as one of creating them, instead it is one of creating a mutually beneficial relationship and helping them to grow and

63

develop.

My intent is to share with you the things which I do and which work for me without any agenda of proposing it as "the way" Some of the protocols and conventions will address specific tenets; others will have an application to more than one; however, all will reflect the tenets to lead and to guide. I use both written and oral methods of teaching based on the paradigm of tell them how to do it, show them how to do it and have them do it. My SOP is a living thing; things are added or subtracted as needed to accomplish the mission. That mission is to create a viable, demonstrable and meaningful experience for everyone involved. My protocols and conventions have been developed out of my military background and are based on the premise that those who are in my household are intelligent subordinates who have made a voluntary choice to serve.

To share my protocols I will lay out the progression which leads to someone joining my household then discuss the ways in which they are expected to conduct themselves.

The process begins with getting to know one another in a variety of settings. This is an informal, no-requirements process establishing an environment of exploration and learning. When an interest is expressed, I share things I have written which reflect some of my philosophy, expectations and requirements. Included with material discussing the dynamics of domination and submission and power exchange relations, are some of the protocols I use; for example, a prescribed set of positions to be used in different settings and rituals. Petitioning to enter service is a key protocol introduced during this period.

The first protocol used to enter my service is to petition to serve. Petitioning to serve is a common convention in most groups and organizations which have a service orientation, be they religious orders or social service ones. Recruiting, if you look closely at it, is more the creation of an awareness of opportunities to serve than it is a selection process. Being drafted to do something removes consent from the equation even if you have some rights of refusal. Drafting is a form of taking, not giving. In a relationship based on a power exchange the offer to relinquish power is the foundation. Exchange by definition is something returned for something given, which in this instance is the acceptance of the obligation of being a master in return for the surrender of personal power. The acceptance of a petition is not to create a conditional status but rather one where a petitioner is to progress through a period of learning the ways of the house to which they are pledged. In the Eastern Orthodox churches as one progress in their learning they are awarded additional vestments at each step. Earning their leathers?

The petition is made first as an oral request by the one desiring to enter service. At this time another protocol is introduced; a formal written petition is provided for the petitioner to learn. There is also a formal written acceptance for the master to use. In an ideal world this is done in a formal ritual form with witnesses but can also be done in private then included as a part of the collaring ceremony. In a poly house I do it in front of the other house members. This will be the first formal use of previously taught positions.

The petition to enter service having been made and accepted is the first step in the pledging and the creation of the relationship. From this point on there is a daily ritual of an affirmation of the pledge with a corresponding acceptance of the pledge. In person this is done in a specific manner including the use of the offering position. However if circumstances require it can be done either in an email or on the telephone. The important thing is that it is always done.

The relationship is created and defined by the petition, acceptance and the pledges of the principals; however, one more step is required to consummate it. The final protocol in the process is the collaring ceremony. The use of a formal collaring ceremony is to share the pledge in a public manner, bearing witness to the pledge we have made to one another. The use of a ritual format demonstrates the importance of the pledges. The ritual protocol for this ceremony consists of five parts and two symbols. The five parts are presentation of the petitioner, the petition, the acceptance, the collaring and a request. The two symbols are a collar and a leash. The petitioner is brought to the master escorted by a respected friend of both individuals and presented as being someone who wishes to petition to enter service. The formal petition is recited using a prescribed format. The master accepts the petition using a format which includes the physical placement of a collar on the petitioner as a symbol of their servitude. When the collar has been placed, the pledged one offers the leash with the request that it be attached to the collar in order that the master can lead and guide them. The pledged and the master recite their affirmations to end the ceremony.

To ensure the spiritual and emotional components of the relationship a variety of everyday protocols are used. These are designed to be subtle so that they do not attract undue attention from persons who are not involved in the master slave lifestyle but are obvious to those who are. The collar being the symbol of the relationship, some form of collar is worn twenty four hours a day. The collar is the physical symbol which identifies the relationship and can take many forms, since it is a symbol and not a defining object. To ensure a collar can be worn everyday and in all situations, each pledged one is provided with a variety of them, mostly in the form of choker necklaces. I select each collar and carry them for a period to infuse them with my energy before placing them on the recipient. A Story of O ring on the third finger of the right hand is also a symbol of the relationship. For formal events a dedicated and obvious ownership collar is worn. One additional protocol involving a collar is the use of a scene collar which will be discussed later.

There are guidelines for conduct which are included in the daily routine and also cover social situations. When attending the master the one attending is always positioned on the left and slightly to the rear when standing, the traditional position of respect assumed by a subordinate. Some form of subtle physical contact is maintained in order to ensure their presence. A position to the left is maintained at all times for example when seated at meals or in a social setting. When introduced the subordinate one will use an action similar to that used in Asia. With the hands in front of the chest, palm to palm with fingers extended, the introduction is acknowledged with a nod of the head.

In social situations, posture and language should always demonstrate personal pride and respect for self as well as respect for all others present. When spoken, to eye contact will be made and maintained as a sign of respect for the speaker, irrespective of their chosen role. Taking on a subordinate role does not deprive that person of their individuality and personality; it only requires that respect be shown to those who have earned it. When not in the presence of the master, modesty and common courtesy are the protocols which are followed. Confronted by inappropriate remarks or requests, the polite statement "that should be addressed to the master" is the response. Trust is a two-way requirement, so the intelligence of the person who has entered into service is to be not only respected but nurtured.

SM scenes have their own set of specific protocols of a ritual nature. I feel that the mental aspect of a scene is critical to its success for both participants, so I use ritual to create it. My premise is that a scene is a reward for service so the ritual is designed with that in mind. The following describes a scene in which the bottom is standing and attached to some form of vertical apparatus.

The first step in the ritual is the use of a scene collar as mentioned above. To begin the bottom uses the offering position to indicate that they are prepared to give themselves over to the scene. The ownership collar, if one is worn, is removed and the scene collar is attached in its place. The use of the scene collar is designed to provide a beginning and an end to the scene: as long as it is in place the scene is in progress. The bottom is still dressed at this point and simply takes a position to one side to either watch the preparations or to reflect and prepare themselves mentally. The tool chest is placed on a stand and the contents removed, uncased and arranged. Since my scenes are unscripted everything in the tool chest is laid out to be available for use. When the tools are arranged, the next step is to prepare the apparatus to be used, arranging the attachments and testing them.

When these preparations are completed I remove my shirt if in a public dungeon or become nude if in a private setting. At this point the bottom is directed to remove all garments and become nude. This is done by gesture in order to maintain the mood. When the bottom is nude the wrist cuffs are displayed, which is the signal to assume the offering position again and have the cuffs put on. The bottom is then raised to a standing position and physical contact is made in the form of an embrace, which is the first physical aspect of the scene. The bottom is lead to the apparatus and attached to the restraint points. The scene then progresses through the four parts of warm up, build up, crescendo and recovery or aftercare. The transition from crescendo to recovery is marked by the protocol of placing a fleece blanket around the bottom, then releasing them from the apparatus used. When the negotiated aftercare has concluded the bottom redresses in some manner and the scene collar is removed. The ownership collar is replaced at this time, if appropriate, since this ritual is also used with those who are not pledged to me.

I use protocols to add an additional level value to our lives together. The daily affirmation of the pledges made by those in the relationship reminds us of our obligations to one another. The rituals, a form of protocol, are used to create and reinforce those spiritual and emotional aspects which are critical to the success of the relationships. Having preset standards creates an environment where people know what is expected and how to conduct themselves.

The dynamics of domination and submission as the basis for interpersonal partnerships are unique in their nature; the use of personal protocols defines each such relationship in a way which sets them apart. Creating protocols which are unique to a relationship is a way of ensuring that the relationship has meaning for the partners. The key to the successful use of protocols in relationships is to make them a living and developing dimension of your journey. As people grow and develop within a relationship they change; protocols need to be flexible to respond to those changes. Living is not a static process; therefore we can not allow the way we live it to become fixed. Do not allow your protocols to be come fixed and stagnant, keep them alive and flexible to potentiate the relationship.

About the Author:

A committed follower of the leather tradition, Sergeant Major has taken on paying forward to those who want to learn in order to repay those who took the time to teach him. Dedicated to preserving the traditions of brotherhood, honesty, trust and loyalty which are the hallmarks of the leather tradition into the 21st Century by sharing them with those who want to go beyond the gateway of the lifestyle. Serving in his community as a teacher, mentor and worker and leading by example as a master. Proud to be honoured by having slave riches pledged to him.

Memberships:
MAsT: Twin Cities
Minnesota Leather Pride Committee
STL3, St Louis
Associate member, Atons of Minneapolis
Associate member, Chicago Leather Club

The Five Unwritten Rules of BDSM

By Cassy Horrocks

I became involved in BDSM when I was 21; I am 53 now. Very soon after meeting the first dominant I ever knew, I was taught the unwritten rules of BDSM and was expected to adhere to those rules or find myself facing consequences.

In recent years I have observed new people joining the ranks of the older, more experienced participants. I welcome their contributions and the fresh ideas that are being introduced with their involvement; sadly however, the unwritten rules don't seem to have been passed down.

I haven't seen the "Unwritten Rules" specifically addressed in quite some time. I suppose by writing of them here they are no longer unwritten, but if we expect to police our own, it's important that people who are serious about being involved know the basics of BDSM etiquette.

There are a variety of explicit rules for specific types of events such as munches, private parties and regional/national events. However, the five basic rules of protocol, those I was taught when I was new to the Scene, are very simple.

1. What you do and see at any event stays at that event.

This is pretty self-explanatory but becomes more difficult as you make more friends who are also involved in the BDSM

69

community. It is perfectly acceptable to discuss your own scene in detail but if you wish to talk about something you have seen others do it is important not to name names. One can say, "At a party I went to I saw a Dominant do... and the submissive responded..." but never mention names or the location you observed the scene. It's tempting when new to the Scene to try to name drop so that others will "know" that you are serious and a real-time participant. Be assured that patience and time will show your commitment level; name-dropping just makes one appear over-eager and impatient. It is also considered the height of bad manners.

2. If you aren't willing to stop a scene perceived to be unsafe, don't mention it later

If you witness something you consider to be unsafe, approach the Dungeon Monitor or the host of the event and bring it to their attention discreetly. It is their responsibility to either point out to you that you are mistaken (many things occur behind the scenes that you may not be aware of) or they will handle the safety issue at hand.

Do not discuss the perceived unsafe act with others who were either present or not present at a later time if you are not prepared to act on your concerns at the time the event takes place. To discuss the activity with others after-the-fact is inappropriate if you stood by and did nothing at the time of the scene.

Even if you did act and discuss the scene with a D.M., see the rule about what happens at an event stays at an event.

3. If you don't know someone and their way of practicing BDSM-D/s, don't infringe upon it physically or through your discussions. Try to learn instead of being judgmental or destructive.

Humiliation play could be one example of a type of play one might find discomfiting. A couple I am acquainted with do extreme humiliation play and at one major event a spectator stepped in to "rescue" the submissive from a perceived "abusive" situation. The D.M. was very familiar with this particular couple and their type of scene and had to remove the do-gooder from the area. This is only one example of being unfamiliar with someone else's style of scening. The fact that one is unfamiliar with a particular style of scene does not necessarily make that style "wrong" or dangerous.

We speak of being accepting of everyone's kink but in a situation where you cannot be accepting, walk away from it and ask questions later, when the couple has had time to recuperate. Most people are more than willing to discuss controversial scenes with those who don't understand. Try to be open minded and learn from new experiences, and remember that at public events safe-words are in place to indicate that the scene should stop; the comfort level of the spectators is not a consideration.

4. Be courteous, show common courtesy and say hello to everyone you can. That is respectful and will earn you courtesy in return. Use titles/honorifics as you see fit through YOUR way of practicing BDSM.

Many people are afraid to say hello at an event because they don't know whether the person they are speaking to is Dom/me or sub. Forget orientation initially, and just say, "Hello, my name is ... and I'm new here." Unless someone points out that they prefer to be addressed as Sir, Ma'am, Goddess or some other title, don't sweat it.

Munches tend to be more casual because they are often in public settings. Over time it will become apparent who is who and as you get to know the people involved you will learn their preferred method of address. In formal settings one may be required to use more formal titles but this will be pointed out in advance. Be observant, watch how others address people and take their lead or just ask how to address them.

Being respectful has absolutely nothing to do with actually respecting someone. It is completely possible to use a respectful tone and form of address without respecting the person being addressed. Behaving in a respectful way says a lot about who YOU are and reflects on your owner if you have one. Your behavior says nothing at all about the other person.

Because someone attend a function, does not give that person "rights." If you are a professed Dominant, you should not expect others to wait on you because they are submissive. A submissive is not required to wait on anyone unless they choose to, and if they choose to they will ask if they may bring a beverage or other refreshment. An offer of refreshment in no way entitles the person being served to any further service, especially sexual service. Never "order" a submissive to do something unless you have that right by virtue of being their Dominant.

5. Do NOT touch any other person or their things without permission.

This rule seems pretty basic but it's the one I most often see disregarded. Hugging seems to be de rigueur at events these days but not everyone enjoys hugging people who are casual acquaintances. A quiet "may I?" with arms open will indicate one wishes to approach for a hug and the willingness of the one being approached will be equally apparent. If the person being greeted is a submissive, permission may be required from their owner rather than from them personally. The submissive concerned will usually indicate whose permission is required.

Touching someone's implements, toys, tools or equipment without first asking permission is the height of rudeness. It is simple to ask, "May I handle that to get a better look at it or feel for it?" Most of the time people are happy to display their belongings but some of them are valuable or quite old and need special care in handling that the owner wants to oversee.

"Unwritten Rules" are not always well-received by those who will insist that there ARE no rules in BDSM, or they don't want to do things the way they USED to be done. That's okay. They're welcome to disregard and behave in any manner they see fit. I do know that in my world if they don't want to follow these simple rules of conduct and insist on behaving badly, their invitation pool will dry up rather rapidly.

The 10 Commandments of Kink
As revealed to Graydancer, Ninja Sex
Poodle & Ronin of Love

By Graydancer

*Apologies to those whose religious beliefs do not have room for
parody, and will therefore be offended by this.*

And it came to pass that in that land there were an abundance
of people who did delight in sharing their kink one with another.

And while it was agreed that their kinks had oft been begotten
by the Old Guard, verily all of their efforts to define that Old Guard
fell like ripe seeds upon barren soil, bearing no fruit and causing
much bitterness and strife and letters to the editor. And as none
were happy with this, they stopped. And much rejoicing was heard
amongst the interwebs.

And while it was generally agreed upon that because of this
nebulousness of form amongst our kinky forebears and foredykes and
foredaddies and foreboys and forebois and thou gettest the idea, it
was also evident to all that certain commonalities did exist among
the communities.

Whereupon it came to pass in the City of Wind, amongst the
flock of the prophet Howie and his many ministers and ministrixes,
a small band of pansexuals did gather together to partake of the
sacraments of sushi.

And amongst this group some did top and some did bottom

and some did both, and there were players of the edge and they who of a surety were newbies, and yet they did dwell together in that place of raw fish and edamame in harmony and laughter.

Verily the sushi was shared by Kimono Boy and Painslut alike, and from the cleansing power of wasabi their minds were collectively opened to revelation.

For while there is no one true way, yet there is still common experience shared by those who do kink in public.

And Ten Commandments were handed down from their collective soylent souls, "commandments" being defined as in any kinky endeavor as agreed upon by those parties consenting to play one with another.

The first of these commandments was caused by the envy of many for the member of their party whose dance card did begin with Saint Claire of Adams that night. And it was rendered thus:

Thou shalt not covet thy neighbors play date.

And the second commandment was inspired by the travails of good Saint Jack McGeorge, who saith,

Thou shalt not out another's kink.

New words were deemed necessary, then, to describe those who sin through disacceptance of another's kink:

Thou shalt not commit judgery.

The fourth commandment, thus:

**Thou shalt honor the safeword and keep it wholly;
Neither shalt thou utter the safeword in vain.**

The fifth commandment was the shortest, needing no explanation:

Ouch is not a safeword.

When thou walkest amongst those who sceneth, remember well the sixth commandment:

Thou shalt not interrupt.

Of two parts was the seventh commandment, each the helpmeet of the other:
*Thou shalt ask for what thou wantith,
And thou shalt get what thou asketh for.*

Many sad and sorrowful words formed the eighth commandment and were put therein:

*Thou shalt not stand in the corner of the dungeon by thyself
and crack thy singletail all night long.*

Verily the seraph Sheryn did find fewer words to fit in the eighth commandment, rendering it thusly:

Thou shalt not be creepy.

With much respect and honor for the past did the ninth commandment come to be:

*Unless thy name be Chuck Renslow or Larry Townsend,
Thou art probably not Old Guard.*

The final commandment of kind was directed to those who believe they are Gods, and have forsaken the knowledge that while that may be true, there have been many Gods before and there will of a surety be many after. The tenth commandment is for all who sceneth:

*Thy ego must fit within a 4,000 square foot dungeon,
Lest it afflict thy fellows with the awful stench
Of unwashed hubris.*

And upon the uttering of the tenth commandment, those assembled were filled with the desire to leave the land of sushi and spread their floggers and cheeks wheresoever the opportunity presenteth, being mindful of the commandments and keeping them wholly.

And it was good.

About the Author:

Graydancer is a kink educator, performer, and activist from the midwest. His writings include the novels <u>Nawashi</u> (available from Lulu.com) and <u>Jujun</u> (podiobooks.com) as well as regular contributions to BestSexBloggers.com. His podcast on rope bondage, Ropecast.net, has been running for over three years with interviews and information on rope, kink, and the occasional pun. He is also the creator of the GRUE: Graydancer's Ropetastic Unconference Extravaganza, a grass-roots kink event which has surfaced in places like St. Louis, Minneapolis, Toronto, and Michigan. More information available at www.graydancer.com .

Manual Creation:
Defining the Structure of an M/s Household

by Machele Kindle (Master Fire)
Reviewed by TammyJo Eckhart

There are two types of rules, protocols or structure books on the market today: those that promote a single way to do things, often called "the one true way" by those denigrating them, and those which offer a specific example while walking the reader through the mind of the creator. <u>Manual Creation: Defining the Structure of an M/s Household</u> by Machele Kindle (Master Fire) is in the second category of these books.

In 8 chapters, Machele Kindle, better known as Master Fire, gives us insights into how she has set up and runs her own M/s household. Most of the chapters have subsections that deal with a particular issue. Each of these gives her own reasoning behind her expectations, a set of introspection activities for both masters and slaves, and finally a copy of the relevant part of her household manual.

Chapter 1 lays out the intended audience and the goals for this book. Primarily, those interested in master-slave or Ds relationships might find it useful. Given that the difference between sub and slave, master and dominant is often more a matter of personal taste than actual roles, expectations or limits, I think it is good to include both categories here.

Kindle has three goals for this book: first, to help readers figure out what they want from their own M/s relationships, and second, to help readers understand themselves better. Frankly I think these two goals are interchangeable; how can we truly know what we want until we understand ourselves? Finally she hopes her readers will understand that these processes are actually ongoing, requiring flexibility and further reflection. Chapter 2 is really an expansion of the third goal by talking about the development of the manual and the individuals supporting it.

The next four chapters detail the various topics covered in Kindle's manual. Chapter 3 covers the basic concepts of contracts, biography, application, collars and tokens, deal breakers, and hierarchies in the household. This is a manual created by the potential master, so all of the sections are from the top's perspective. However, I agree with Kindle that anyone considering serving another needs to get as much information as possible before making that decision. I strongly recommend that future slaves read these sections and consider all the thought that goes into setting up a household.

Chapter 4 is the bulk of the book because it deals with the actual day-to-day living requirements for someone in the House of Fire. Several things seem repetitive here, but when we are setting up structures to live with I think repetition is helpful, and it certainly clarifies what is important to individual masters and their households.

Similar to the previous chapter, chapter 5 lays out what the potential master has to offer those who enter her house. By wording things slightly differently the feeling is one of an extended résumé like one might offer to a prospective employer. Some of you may bristle at the idea that the dominant is being interviewed as much as the submissive is, but I thoroughly agree with Kindle that it is best for the top to be clear about what they can and will offer in return for service.

Chapter 6 is an explanation of some closing statements that can help conclude your household manual. My own household structure is based on my training manual, which does not include such a closing statement. I'm not sure how I feel about the idea, but this short chapter did get me to think about it. Chapter 7 is really just one page, encouraging the reader to start writing down what they want and start the process of their own manual creation.

Chapter 8 is really just the manual in its full form without commentary from Kindle. It felt a bit redundant, given the citation of sections in the preceding chapters. However, many readers may want to see what a household manual looks like, so for them this is a good addition. I liked that at the end of each page there was a space for both potential master and slave to note that they have read and discussed the manual. Too often people jump into their relationships without fully understanding what is expected from each partner; this leads to hurt feelings and greater difficulties later on.

The five appendices that conclude the book are greater details about some matters in the manual, such as presentation forms, lists of other sources the reader might want to consult, and some quotations from books or articles Kindle has found inspiration from. As always, be aware that online references can and do change quickly.

Kindle does a good job of letting us inside her mind as she walks us through her only household manual. The introspection activities at the end of each section are well placed and ask helpful questions. Her overwhelmingly positive and realistic approach is refreshing in a world where too many people try to tell others how they must live their own lives. The best way for your relationship to work is a way that makes it beneficial for everyone involved.

PEBRS

80

The Owner's Manual: A Comprehensive Handbook for the BDSM Community and D/s Relationships

by Rusty Haway
Reviewed by TammyJo Eckhart

I've been asked to list the "best" books on the market today for BDSM. With a miniature flood of general books this can be a daunting task. But non-fiction books about Ds or dominance and submission in its multitude of varieties are much rarer to find. One such book is Rusty Haway's The Owner's Manual: A Comprehensive Handbook for the BDSM Community and D/s Relationships.

The founder of what is now called the HOH, a pansexual group in Houston, Texas, writes this book. Why do I mention this? Because, while the website for the group makes it sound very friendly and welcoming, that is not the tone of this manual. Immediately this book has negative things to say about what it terms "pansexual" or "new guard" BDSM (pp. 4-9) — frankly, I don't think these are necessarily synonymous terms.

Likewise, while the book urges its readers to have an open mind, its stated goals suggest a lack of such. These three goals (p. 4) are: 1) remove vanilla thinking, 2) make the individual a stronger dominant or submissive, and 3) form a "national uniformity code of conduct." Number two is great — don't we all want to be the best we can be?

But what is "vanilla thinking?" We say the term "vanilla,"

but usually it's defined simply as non-kinky. Haway really needs to be very clear about what "vanilla thinking" is and why it should be removed.

The third goal is completely unrealistic. First, Haway uses a percentage, 10%, as the amount of Ds people in the kinky community. Where does he get this number? I've seen some studies of kinky people, and they aren't very good, either because they have a therapeutic approach, meaning that we only hear about people with problems, or because they have a volunteer approach, where members of kinky organizations and professionals respond to a survey or are interviewed. Both of these are far from objective or representational of any general kinky community.

I've known a good number of kinky people, but none of them have subscribed to the same theory or method in their relationships. Why should they? What would be the benefit? Some benefit needs to be shown to me first before I'll starting changing how my household works.

Throughout the book there are excellent insights and positive suggestions for improving communication, building a solid Ds foundation, and helping each person get better in a particular role. Overall the manual is poorly organized, jumping from one point to another, and sometimes contradicts itself, such as when it states the idea that Ds isn't "play" and yet invites us to "play" the Ds game (pp. 4, 9). I'll list some of the sections and topics covered in The Owner's Manual, because I think they hold potential to cover many important topics that fall into the Ds realm.

A little bit of history will almost always entice me. However, Haway really needs to cite his "facts," not only because that is what any decent historical work does, but also because it seems to contradict some information I've picked up through the years.

Almost all of his suggestions for safety and personal insight while looking for a partner show that Haway has taken the time to study human beings and what makes their relationships thrive. The focus seems to be on male-dominant and female-submissive seekers, but that is Haway's personal experience, and it is good either to write from your experience or to do a lot of research.

Protocol is a tricky concept, and few books try to explain how they work and what they cover. Part of chapter four and most of chapter five give very solid examples of areas in which protocols may be appropriate and why they can be helpful. The trick here is to see the examples as merely that: examples from Haway's own life, not models to be blindly used.

This handbook makes a rather lofty claim of being "comprehensive" and falls far short of that goal. May I give a general piece of advice to all authors out there? Steer clear of terms like "comprehensive," "complete," "authoritative," and other words that imply such perfection. Odds are very high that you will fail if you claim to be so thorough.

At the end of the book (p. 79), Haway asks for suggestions, because he plans to revise this manual every six months. While my review has not been glowing and indeed is quite harsh at times, it is my hope that The Owner's Manual: A Comprehensive Handbook for the BDSM Community and D/s Relationships will be revised in a very serious fashion before its next edition. There is potential here, but the potential is not realized in the 2001 edition. This edition needs to be reorganized and edited by people outside of the HOH community, where perhaps they have reached a wider consensus on a code of conduct.

Protocol Handbook for the Leather Slave: Theory and Practice

by Robert J. Rubel, PhD
Reviewed by TammyJo Eckhart

It is rather ironic that after receiving a few emails from folks looking for protocol books, I received this book to review. Robert J. Rubel's <u>Protocol Handbook for the Leather Slave: Theory and Practice</u> is part guidebook and part personal manual for his household. What can it offer the reader as a guide to master-slave relationships?

<u>Protocol Handbook</u> has six chapters in which to describe some of the theory and practice of a master-slave relationship. From the introduction onward, Rubel never claims that his way is the way his readers should do things. He has strong opinions about what may be a good approach and experience with the situations that arise, but he is comfortable and confident enough in his household that he need not attempt to recreate it in other places.

Rubel does not just rely on his own experiences, protocol or rules that govern what the master expects of the slave. He draws from other successful master-slave structures that he has heard of and seen. While he uses a male master and female slave model (this is how his house is structured) his basic ideas and questions, all of the experiences he draws from, cross gender and sexual orientation lines well. If you read this and are unclear at any point about what Rubel's manual says, he has provided ample commentary on passages.

Rubel also distinguishes between the dominant-submissive

relationship, where power is exchanged, and the master-slave relationship, where authority is exchanged. I'm sure many will disagree with these categories (as they will with his distinction between BDSM and Leather), but I personally feel a similar way, though for different reasons. All these basic terms and concepts are discussed in chapter 1.

Chapter 2 is a short chapter that looks at how masters and slaves interact in social spaces — vanilla, kinky, and in relationships with others as friends and family. The basics are expanded on in chapter 3, where Rubel gives specific examples of how he expects his slave to behave in various situations. As you read this you may be struck with how much thought and detail he's gone into — he has covered what is important to him; if it does not match you, determine other protocols. The point is to have rules that flow for you and make your master-slave relationship functional and positive.

Chapter 4 looks a bit more closely at how Rubel's slave is to interact with him one-on-one. This may be in the privacy of his home or in a more vanilla setting, such as a restaurant. Having a protocol can turn any seemingly vanilla situation into another structured part of a master-slave dynamic without drawing unnecessary or unwanted attention.

Chapter 5 is the chapter I can least relate to. Here are rules and routines that Rubel has trained and expects his own slave to follow. I know that other households have similar arrangements, but frankly some of us don't. As I read through them I could see that these were expectations from a different economic and social class from the one I myself was raised in. Again, there is nothing here that says, "This is the one true way," so while I felt a bit put off by the degree of specificity, I did not feel chided or directed.

Chapter 6 looks further at the role of a slave as the personal assistant for the master. In Rubel's house this includes maid, valet, chef, secretarial, and courtesan services. I noticed that the chef, secretarial and courtesan sections are less detailed, probably because these require greater versatility in action. Having sex the exact same way may get boring, but being specific about how often to clean the house is wise management.

After some closing thoughts the book ends with six appendices that cover various concepts that have come up in the book. There are also a select group of resources that both the reader and Rubel's slave can use to investigate topics or do a better job.

I couldn't run my house in the way Rubel does. I don't have the same social and economic background that would make his own protocols comfortable or functional for me. His way does not need to be my way, though, and at no time does Rubel claim that it should be. That is the main reason why I really love this book. It offers solid advice and shows us a real-life model, but never claims to be the best way or the only way to structure your relationship.

PROTOCOLS
Handbook for the female slave

Robert J. Rubel, PhD

Master/slave Relations:
Handbook of Theory and Practice

Robert J. Rubel, PhD
Foreword by Jay Wiseman, JD

Purchase from www.PowerExchangeBooks.com

Master/slave Relations

COMMUNICATIONS 401
THE ADVANCED COURSE

Robert J. Rubel, PhD

Purchase from www.PowerExchangeBooks.com

Master/slave Relations

SOLUTIONS 402
LIVING IN HARMONY

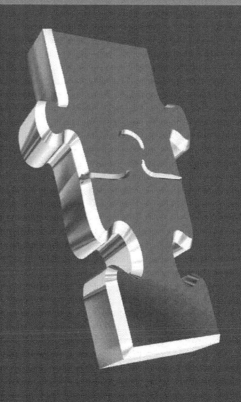

Robert J. Rubel, PhD

Robert J. Rubel, PhD
Foreword by Jay Wiseman

Squirms, Screams and Squirts

Now you can turn great sex into extraordinary sex

#1 recommended book for
Valentines' Day 2008 by
Playboy Online

To be reviewed in the Valentines' Day issue of
Penthouse Forum 2009

Purchase from www.PowerExchangeBooks.com

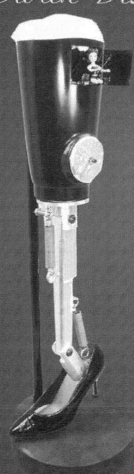

Power Exchange Books

Playing with Disabilities

Robert J. Rubel, PhD, Series Editor
Angela Stassinopoulos, Issue Coordinator

Purchase from www.PowerExchangeBooks.com

Purchase from www.PowerExchangeBooks.com

List of New Resource Books for the End of 2008 and all of 2009

- Age Play

- Anal Fisting and Power Exchange

- Bears and their Cubs

- Dominance and submission in 24/7 Relationships -- some observations

- Dressed to Kill

- Leatherdykes -- Multiple Perspectives   Sent confirming letter 9/7/08

- Leather Ethics

- Leather Protocols – a variety of views

- Love Issue, The

- Medical Play

- On Power and Domination

- Rope Bondage and Power Exchange (sent to Lee 9/8/08)

- Spirituality and Bootblacking

- SM tools and Power exchange

- Tea Service

- Transgendered/transsexual

Titles in Search of Authors

If you are interested in contributing to any of these issues, please contact me at: PowerExchangeEditor@Yahoo.com

Please say: "Interested in Writing" in the subject line.

› About Power

› Aging M/s Couple, The

› After your Title Year

› Book for submissives, The

› Birth and Training of a Leather Master, The

› BDSM and People of Color

› Book for submissives, The

› Bringing in the Next Generation

› Cigar Play

› Coming Out Kinky: The Joys and Sorrows

› Dressed to Kill: fetish dressing in the world of BDSM

› Exploitation vs Ownership in the M/s Relationship

› Family, Kids, and Kink — Some Challengers

› Finding your Path

› From the Internet to Real Time

› Generational Differences Affecting BDSMers

› Giving Back

› Gorean Relationships

› How to Collect Men

- › In Search of Master
- › Leadership
- › Leather, What is...
- › Long-term M/s Relationships -- what keeps them together
- › Mentoring — Giving and Receiving
- › Multiple Service Relationships
- › Objectification
- › Physiology – Understanding how the Human Body Responds to SM play
- › Prose -- a Collection of Kinky Works
- › Symbols, The Importance of
- › Shaping Your Power
- › Tats, Body Modification, and Scarification
- › Transgendered/transsexual
- › Vampirism
- › What Makes a Master?

Power Exchange Books'
Resource Series
can be purchased at
www.PowerExchangeBooks.com

» Playing with Disabilities

» The Art of Slavery

» Protocols – A Variety of Views